Praise for McMillan's work

"McMillan's expressive style...al of thoughtful rage."
— *Comics Journal*

"Very talented."
— *Washington Post*

"Razor-sharp critique packaged as cute-kid-and-funny-animal cartoon."
— *Booklist*

"This is social satire at its wittiest and most engaging."
— Howard Zinn, author of *A People's History of the United States*

"...like oxygen for our suffocating times."
— Vandana Shiva, author of *Soil Not Oil*

"Provocative, insightful, and entertaining."
— Jeff Monson ("The Snowman"), world champion mixed martial arts fighter

"...unflinchingly confront(s) these pressing issues, and the book is really funny too..."
— Andy Hurley, drummer for Fall Out Boy

"Visionary and honest."
— Ted Rall, cartoonist, author of *To Afghanistan and Back*

"Her politics are perfect, her drawings sly and subtle, and her dialog funny as hell."
— Derrick Jensen, author of *Endgame*

"The cartoon generated a huge amount of filth, intolerable filth."
— former Senator Bill Napoli (R-SD), sponsor of abortion ban *(Rapid City Journal)*

ALSO BY STEPHANIE MCMILLAN

The Minimum Security Chronicles: Resistance to Ecocide
(2013, Seven Stories Press)

The Beginning of the American Fall: A Comics Journalist Inside the Occupy Wall Street Movement
(2012, Seven Stories Press)

The Knitting Circle Rapist Annihilation Squad
(2012, PM Press, with Derrick Jensen)

Mischief in the Forest
(2010, PM Press, with Derrick Jensen)

As the World Burns: 50 Simple Things You Can Do to Stay in Denial
(2007, PM Press, with Derrick Jensen)

Attitude Presents: Minimum Security
(2005, NBM Publishing)

Anthologies:

World War 3 Illustrated, #45: Before and After
(2014)

The Graphic Canon, Volume 3: The World's Greatest Literature as Comics
(2013, Seven Stories Press)

Stay Solid: A Radical Handbook for Youth
(2013, AK Press)

Earth At Risk: Building a Resistance Movement to Save the Planet
(2013, Flashpoint Press)

Excessive Force
(2009, Last Hours, UK)

Attitude: The New Subversive Political Cartoonists
(2002, NBM Publishing)

CAPITALISM MUST DIE!

**A basic introduction to capitalism:
what it is,
why it sucks,
and how to crush it.**

Stephanie McMillan

Discounts available for distributors or bulk orders.

ISBN: 978-0-9916047-0-8

A full-color digital version is also available at stephaniemcmillan.org. A condensed version is available as a Powerpoint slide show and video.

Support for the author's writing/comics/organizing is appreciated! (Landlords and grocery stores haven't yet repudiated capitalism). Paypal: steph@minimumsecurity.net

Stephanie McMillan
P.O. Box 460673
Fort Lauderdale, FL 33346

More information: stephaniemcmillan.org
Contact: steph@minimumsecurity.net

This is a publication of Ideés Nouvelles, Ideés Prolétairiennes.
koleksyon-inip.org

10 9 8 7 6 5 4 3 2 1
Printed in the USA

May 1, 2014

Idées Nouvelles
Idées Prolétariennes

This is dedicated to all who seek
a path to collective emancipation.

Heartfelt thanks to my comrades:
near and far, known and unknown.

CONTENTS

Extras:

INTRODUCTION

From the Publisher

INIP (Idées Nouvelles Idées Prolétariennes/New Ideas Proletarian Ideas) is a publishing entity for the popularization of theory that serves the interests of the working class in the struggle against capital.

No theory, ideas, or definition of theory (philosophy) can exist outside class struggle. They are, in fact, determined and produced by class struggle. Even when those ideas and theories are initiated by individuals, they ultimately and objectively elevate to a class line. They articulate a class interest, for the sole purpose of class reproduction and advancement based on an alternative.

Proletarian class consciousness is a crucial element of a revolutionary struggle, along with proletarian organization, and exists in dialectical relation with (determined by) practice. Proletarian class consciousness is currently at an extreme ebb in most social formations, one aspect of an overall extremely unfavorable balance of forces in the current historical period. Corresponding to this, we are witnessing a widespread ossification and stagnation of proletarian revolutionary theory.

Proletarian theory, with Marxism-Leninism as its foundation, has historically accomplished an objective in the consolidation and definition of proletarian theory (which many others have contributed to as well), and simultaneously of a political line against the most antagonistic enemy of the proletariat: capital (and the capitalist class) in the most advanced stage of imperialism. Marxism marks the triumph of a theory and a political orientation over others at a particular stage in the development of capitalism, and Leninism marks the triumph of proletarian theory at the stage of imperialism. We are still in the same period; class struggle hasn't brought us to a new stage, as other political trends have declared. The fundamental contradiction is still between capital and labor. But in this stage of imperialism, Marxism-Leninism has reached period of maturity as the foundation of proletarian theory, and it is now necessary to make this theory the collective property of the working class.

It is also necessary to demarcate from the current recuperation and distortion of proletarian theory by a section of the petit bourgeoisie, who is becoming radicalized during the current crisis of capitalism, in response to losing stability. (Occupy was essentially an expression of outrage in reaction to this decline in position, and resistance to proletarianization). This has resulted in a Left that is largely dominated by their petit bourgeois interests, and is consequently mired in sectarianism, dogmatism, opportunism and populism.

The petit bourgeoisie has a notion of private property based on their own material conditions: they don't own anything, nor do they produce surplus (exchange) value, but are involved in the circulation of capital. Because of the ideological effects of this relationship to production, they have come to view their own individuality as their only private property. In this period of crisis, they seek alternatives that correspond to their specific class demands (such as liberty and equality). Thus the radical petit bourgeoisie, though well-intentioned, are attempting to claim Marxism-Leninism as their own private property, by identifying their struggle and interests (particularly those of non-productive laborers and service employees) as the struggle and interests of the working class. By conflating these two distinct classes (though both are dominated by capital), they are effectively erasing the working class struggle, and its intermediate objective of proletarian dictatorship.

The petit bourgeoisie is a non-autonomous class, historically incapable of offering an alternative to capitalism. They must ally with either of the two fundamental classes. Normally they side with the bourgeoisie, but as they are squeezed harder by capitalism, they are pushed toward attempting to ally with capitalism's fundamental enemy, the proletariat. In the process, they gravitate toward and appropriate Marxism-Leninism as their own (whether they call it "communism" or anything else), but deform it (this is revisionism) to serve their own class interests.

So in the final analysis their ultimate, underlying objective is for the reproduction of capitalism, not its defeat. The fact that this includes some enlargement of bourgeois democratic rights does make them progressive in some instances. But overall, these tendencies and urges of the petit bourgeoisie are to the great detriment of the fusion of proletarian theory with working class struggle. Now historically, we are facing the total bankruptcy and failure of the leadership of the radical petit bourgeoisie in the international struggle, which has consolidated the ossification and stagnation of proletarian theory.

In contrast, we insist on the need for the working class to lead its own struggle, in its interests. Proletarian theory has been constructed in, and is a guide to, our struggle against capital. Only when the proletariat appropriates its theory, can it accomplish its historical task of leading the struggle to emancipate the world from capital, and achieve its objective final goal: the abolition of private property. Toward this end, we are attempting to advance and assert proletarian theory for a proletarian line. During this period of imperialism, we must elevate proletarian theory to become the collective property of the INTERNATIONAL WORKING CLASS.

How does this orientation manifest in reality?

1) It simultaneously allows us to construct (based on the dialectical relation of a never ending process of general to specific and specific to general for the elevation of our theory) a PROLETARIAN ALTERNATIVE.

9

2) Proletarian theory/proletarian alternatives are in a constant mode of rectification and consolidation, based on the centralization of three elements: experiences, actual practices, and knowledge. This enables our class and its most advanced detachment (the proletarian revolutionaries) to objectively learn from each other in the dialectical relation of theory and practice, for the validation of our theory and its constant development as a guide to practice.

3) All contributions, even contributions made by petit bourgeois intellectuals and revolutionaries, are the collective property of our class, the working class: to learn from, to demarcate from, and to unite with.

4) We dispense with sectarian labels identifying this theory with any particular individuals ("Maoism," "Trotskyism" etc.), and identify it instead as the theory of a class, forged in the struggle of the proletariat in its interests, to achieve its dual objectives: the defeat of capital, and the dictatorship of the proletariat (the latter condensing and determining the dialectical relationship between them).

This book *Capitalism Must Die!* though attributed to an individual, with corresponding limitations, is a product of our ongoing collective struggle to consolidate the theory of our class and assert a corresponding political line. It is part of the collective property of the working class. This is the reason INIP has chosen to publish it.

— by the revolutionary proletarian nucleus leading INIP
January 9, 2014

PURPOSE & PREMISES

The purpose of this project is to contribute to a collective process of analyzing our objective conditions and clarifying concepts in service to the struggle to defeat capitalism. It rests on, and elaborates, several basic premises.

Premises:

• The capitalist system is evil and omnicidal. It needs to stop.

• It will not disappear or collapse by itself. If allowed to continue, it will devour all life on Earth.

• Capitalism can only be eliminated by overthrowing it in a collective revolutionary process. It can not be reformed out of existence, escaped, or replaced from within.

• Capitalism is a continuously expanding mode of production. Capital struggles for its own self-reproduction. Capitalists accumulate surplus value, which is converted into more capital, through the exploitation of workers as they convert the natural world into commodities.

• The fundamental contradiction of capitalism is capital vs. labor. Its manifestation is the social relationship of domination of one class (workers) by another (capitalists). Its expression is class struggle.

• The working class, or proletariat, is in an antagonistic and strategic position in relation to capital. In liberating itself, it liberates all the dominated classes.

• The proletariat is the only class able to offer an alternative to capitalism. All other classes will tend to reproduce it or some other form of class society.

• In the current crisis of global capitalism, objective conditions are ripening for revolution, but subjectivity (ideology, or consciousness) is lagging, weakening popular mass struggles.

• In order to fulfill its historical mission, the proletariat must become class conscious and appropriate its own theory, which is the synthesized knowledge gained from its own struggles.

• Theory is collectively constructed in the process of class struggle. It can't develop separate from practice. In the dialectical relationship between theory and practice, practice is primary and determinate. Theory is for the purpose of practice, to transform social relations.

There is, of course, a rich body of revolutionary theory of great breadth and depth that is being added to every day. It's impossible for anyone to keep up with it all. So why am I bothering with this project?

My three goals are as follows:

1) To introduce and popularize some basic concepts and ideas, in accessible terms, that may assist others in their current practice or in becoming active participants in the struggle.

2) To use and offer it as an organizing tool (which can be used in various venues including online, in-person presentations, and group discussion).

3) To further my own clarity. I find great insights in the work of others, but I understand ideas better if I relate them to my own experience and write them down in my own words.

Some points on method:

1) This is not an academic exercise or an artist's self-expression. I'm doing this in the service of revolution, and for no other reason. Theoretical clarity for its own sake is pointless intellectualism; instead it should be a guide for action.

2) What I write represents my current (necessarily limited and incomplete) interpretation of reality, which is constantly developing. No one's understanding or ability to communicate can ever keep up with the rate of change of reality itself.

3) No individual can comprehend all the aspects of how society works or how it can be transformed, or precisely what future new forms it may take. No group, even, can comprehend it. Reality can only be fully appropriated by a class as it emerges and defines itself through struggle. The precise path of transforming society cannot be predicted in advance, but only perceived through the act of transforming it.

4) I may revise my work at any time. It is dated according to its latest revision.

5) I'm producing this as an individual (and take all responsibility for mistakes), but it is the product of a collective and historical process. Theory is shaped by revolutionary militants past and present, and we build on the work of those who have come before us. Karl Marx laid the foundation of proletarian theory with his analysis of capital. Countless others have since contributed to it.

6) Constructing theory and organization are intertwined, and I participate directly in organized collective discussion of theory. That includes this specific work. It is not my property.

7) Ideas, like history and everything else, advance through struggle. Feedback, including (especially!) constructive criticism, is always welcome and appreciated.

KNOW the ENEMY

CAPITALISM is The current dominant mode of production and manifestation of class society. It is omnicidal.

PART 1:
KNOW THE ENEMY

GMO MARKETING PLAN

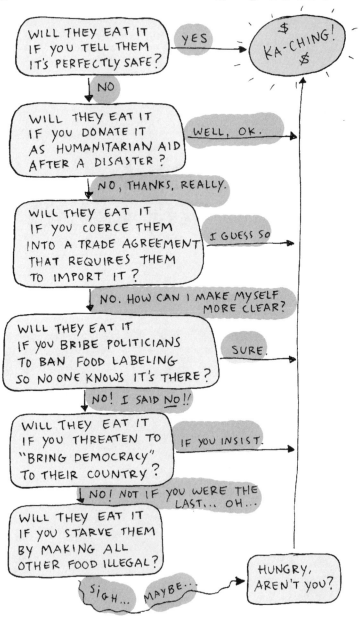

Capitalism is evil

Capitalism is the dominant mode of production in the world to-day, the legacy and current manifestation of about 10,000 years of class-divided society. During the past 500 years it has overtaken other forms of production and developed into an integrated global economy that subjugates every aspect of contemporary life.

The nature of capitalism is omnicidal. This is not simply a moral failing or a mistake: it's built into the mechanism of how it functions. (This is unfortunate—if it were a moral failing, it might be possible to persuade those who run it to stop).

Global capitalism, as an ordinary, integral part of its functioning, annually kills 10 million children under age five because it's not profitable to save them.[1] As part of its normal functioning, it has cut down 78 percent of old-growth forests. It kills 100,000 people in the US annually because it's not profitable to provide them with adequate health care. It has wiped out 93 percent of the large ocean fish. 300,000 people die each year due to climate change.[2] 200 or more entire species become extinct every single day.

Untold millions of dead are its direct victims. The direction of global capitalism is clear: increasing hunger, sorrow, misery and death for the majority, while a few bloated parasites feed off the life-energy of the world. Profit is a cruel imperative.

Capitalism has lost its right to exist.

---

[1] Most of these children die from easily preventable and treatable causes such as birth complications, diarrhea, pneumonia, measles and malnutrition. *State of the World's Mothers 2008: Closing the Survival Gap for Children Under 5*, Save the Children.

[2] Pablo Solón, Bolivia's ambassador to the UN, Democracy Now, December 6, 2010.

Global capitalism is a system

It dominates society economically, ideologically, and politically. It shapes what we think, the ways we spend our time, our moods, our hairstyles, which TV shows we find amusing, whether we prefer popsicles or strawberries, the colors of our t-shirts, who we love, and how we die.

Each social formation is defined by its mode of production (the way the society as a whole meets its needs, how it reproduces itself from one day to the next). The current dominant mode of production is capitalism.

Our livelihoods have been threaded into this system, this giant social machine, like so many wires and tubes, so that we have become as dependent upon it as it is upon us. Mechanics called politicians are appointed to keep the colossus oiled and functioning smoothly. They hire economists to tell them how to do it. They promote culture that pacifies its billions of victims. It hires police and armies to protect it when its victims become disgruntled.

This exploitation machine has taken over all our lives and spans the globe. It converts human labor and the natural world into surplus value, in the pursuit of profit. A few people own it. The rest of us are its fuel.

Its complexity has become a liability to itself, and abrupt simplification is immanent. It's about to downsize, hard. Some people hope and pray for its collapse. But it will not collapse. The machine will be simplified, but it will still run.

Unless we destroy it, capitalism will destroy the world.

The class in power has many methods to enforce our obedience. It uses physical means, such as controlling our basic needs of food and shelter. Social structures — the nuclear family and the fracturing of community — keep us scrambling for survival in isolated units. Laws thwart us every time we turn around. They keep us mired in piles of paperwork. They use the strategy of "divide and rule" very effectively, so we attack one another rather than our common enemy. They divert us into false solutions such as elections and activism for its own sake. They use the media and culture to whip up our outrage over secondary issues so that we fail to address our fundamental problem. They entertain, frighten, and lie to us. They overmedicate us, and poison us with chemicals so we feel like we're playing Russian Roulette every time we eat a meal. They push religion as the Prozac of the masses, and high-tech toys as the meth.

Their most dangerous weapon of all, which they employ freely, is their monopoly on violence. They attack us from all sides. To live in a system of domination is to live in a constant state of violence.

Capitalism corrupts all social relations. It pulls everyone in a reactionary direction. It forces workers to compete against one another. This fosters sexism, racism, nativism and nationalism. It also forces workers, in order to survive, to be situated in opposition to the natural world. This leads to loggers fighting environmentalists, oil drillers and coal miners demanding more jobs even though the effects of this production is to poison all of us and our families. It pits us against our own allies and puts us at war with our own selves. It has countless methods of manipulating and coercing us to serve them, our common enemy, instead.

Because they create dependency, like addicts we throw away our long-term interests for short-term needs. Capitalists have deliberately, fiendishly, cleverly set up our lives this way.

They super-exploit some, like immigrants, and workers in the most dominated countries, so workers living in the imperialist centers can't compete. It's similar to the way capitalists dump grain to make small farmers lose their land. They set the price, and divide us from our own livelihoods. We are led to blame the wrong people for this, to create enemies out of fellow victims.

Emancipating ourselves from this global nightmare must be our highest priority. Everything we do must serve this goal.

Capitalism has a beginning, a long and complicated trajectory still in process, and an end that has yet to come. We need to help bring the end into being. It won't go away by itself.

For decades, a serious weakness in the struggles for social change, including the environmental and social justice movements, has been a lack of understanding of the true nature of the system that we live under, and its economic, political and ideological components. This has resulted in an inability to name capitalism as the problem. Instead we often hear vague populist terms like "The 1%," "the rich," "banksters," and "greedy corporations." But the problem goes much deeper than the depravity of any particular individuals or institutions. It lies in the structural foundation of the entire way of life that currently dominates the globe.

Before we can explore our way out of a problem, we need to come to a common understanding of what the problem is. We need to comprehend the structured processes and relationships that determine why we live the way we do. We need to describe how the system arose and developed, and how it functions, before we can define a political line capable of undermining it and hastening its end.

Though we live enmeshed within capitalism, many people don't know what it is or how it actually functions. We have to understand *why* it's structurally impossible to reform, so that we can deal with the necessity — and our responsibility — not to fix it (because domination and exploitation are built into it from the start) but to do away with it, and to figure out all that will entail. Because of rapidly worsening global warming and the total toxification of the environment, we may in fact be the last generation with the opportunity to do this.

Any form or mode of production converts natural materials into new value (use value, or simply usefulness). Capitalism is a particular mode of production that not only produces new use value, but in that process it also produces *surplus* value, which is embodied in commodities. Surplus value is the result, the residue, of the exploitation of labor. It comprises a portion of the commodity's exchange value, making it profitable to sell. Though our entire society has been structured around obtaining it, it's rarely discussed. We will define and examine it in the upcoming section on commodities.

Under capitalism, one section of people—a small minority comprising an economic class—dominates all others. They are called the capitalist class, or the bourgeoisie. The capitalists monopolize the means of production (which includes the means of subsistence). Others (the working class, otherwise known as the proletariat) are forced to sell their labor power to survive.

The working class produces everything in society, while the capitalist class privately appropriates (in other words: takes...in *other* other words: steals) the products of their labor.

Economic class divisions emerged roughly in tandem with agriculture and the ability of social formations to accumulate surpluses of necessities (wealth). The foundation for these divisions existed even earlier than this, in trade between different social formations, and the gender-based division of labor. From the beginning, class-divided economies have been organized around the private appropriation of accumulated wealth, accomplished through the production of storable, exchangeable goods—salt, spices, grains, cloth, furs, and so on.

Under capitalism these goods have assumed the commodity form, and that exchange value has become distinct from (yet still connected to—extremely tenuously in many cases) use value.

Brief definitions

Social formation: a coherent group system that reproduces itself in a constant dynamic of construction and destruction. It is comprised of the total ensemble or matrix of all its internal contradictions—its structures, processes and relationships (each with its intertwined economic, political, and ideological aspects).

A social formation is defined largely by its dominant mode of production.

Mode of production: the way a social formation is organized to reproduce its own relations of production and productive forces. There are many variations of several basic types:

- **Subsistence-based** (includes hunting and foraging, forest gardening, pastoralism).

- **Slavery** (wealth is obtained by directly forced labor).

- **Feudalism** (serfs or peasants must turn over a portion of their crops to the landowner).

- **Capitalism** (owners of the means of production privately appropriate the commodified labor power of workers).

- **Socialism** (a transition stage during which production is controlled by the working class, and performed to meet society's needs rather than to accumulate private wealth).

- **Communism** (production is engaged in voluntarily for the collective good).

- **Anarchism** (production is engaged in, or not, voluntarily, without the transition period of socialism).

Forms/stages of capitalism:

- **Colonialism** (capitalists expand beyond national limits by conquering and directly administering other social formations to extract resources, exploit labor power, and expand markets).

- **Imperialism** (the internationalization of monopoly capital; the globalization of production through the export not only of goods, but of capital itself).

These are extremely brief and limited abstract concepts, theoretical models which are distinct from historically specific realities. No social formation can be a pure form of one type, and each social formation is different.

As different modes of production become dominant, they don't automatically erase the previous modes; each contains the seeds of the future and elements of the past. They exist in constantly shifting proportions and potentialities. A mode now in decline can later become dominant once again.

Some of these are slightly more elaborated upon in the last section, "Brief Definitions of Concepts."

WE'RE ALL MIDDLE CLASS, AREN'T WE?

A common conception of economic classes is that they are determined by income: rich, middle class and poor. (Secondary qualities related to this viewpoint are education level, institutional power, and social status). The majority in the US thinks of themselves as middle class, whether or not that's true even within this erroneous framework.

This sociological approach to class is promoted by capitalists, because it hides the relationship of domination that actually exists. We can't destroy a system when we don't understand its structure and our place in it. It's impossible to defeat a dominating class if we don't even perceive them as such.

The promotion of the concept of the "middle class" is an ideological act of aggression by the bourgeoisie to deny the class polarization inherent in capitalism (and to deny the existence of classes themselves). Their aim is to reinforce their own class dominance by making it invisible. The myth of the "middle class" erases class struggle.

Classes in fact are defined by their relationship to production. Who owns the means of production? Who produces value, and who profits from it? Who controls the process and the products? The answers to these questions determine one's class position in a society.

Classes exist through their constant struggle to survive, to reproduce themselves within the context of the structural conflict between them. Classes are the effect, the result, the embodiment of the social relations of domination that are continuously generated by the prevailing form of economic activity.

Between the main contending classes in the slavery mode of production (owners and slaves), it is obvious which class dominates the other. Between the main contending classes in the feudal mode of production (landowners and serfs), it is easy to see which class has control. But under capitalism, the relationship between the main contending classes (capitalists and workers) is obscured.

Exploitative social relationships are mediated and concealed by the marketplace, by the buying and selling of objects. The myth of the market is that free agents exchange commodities of equal value, in the form of money, goods, and labor power. (This illusion of capitalism as relations between things rather than between people is what Marx meant by "commodity fetishism.")

In fact, the capitalist class, using its economic, political and ideological hegemony, dominates every aspect of these transactions, employing coercion and exploitation to ensure their own profit at the expense of everyone else.

Basic breakdown of classes under capitalism

These are extremely brief and general descriptions. Classifications have limited correspondence to the complexity of reality. Still, they can be practically useful. There is in fact overlap, movement and blurring between classes, particularly at both ends of the petit bourgeoisie (which is stratified over a very broad range). There are various fractions of each class, with specific secondary characteristics. There is much disagreement about the precise limits and boundaries of each category, as well, and thus about who is included within each.

That said, it is clear that capitalist society is divided into two broad camps: those who own and control the means of production, and everyone else who is dominated by their system: the popular masses, which include the working class plus sections of the petit-bourgeoisie and lumpen proletariat. The fundamental contending classes are the capitalist class and the working class.

Dependent family members are considered to belong to the same class as the main household economic agent.

The capitalist class (or bourgeoisie):

These are the people who own the means of production and distribution, and/or control the process through which capital self-expands. They are the beneficiaries of the productive process. They acquire and accumulate the surplus value created through resource extraction and labor exploitation (as well as gaining profits through trade, rent, interest, and speculation). Those who benefit by representing this class are also effectively members of it.

They include:

- Owners, executives and major shareholders of large companies and corporations
- Large property owners
- Major money lenders: bankers, investors and financiers
- Drug lords
- High-level managers (representatives of capital in the economic realm)
- High-level politicians (representatives of capital in the political realm)
- High-level mainstream media functionaries (representatives of capital in the ideological realm)

The working class (or proletariat):

In short, this class generates surplus value in the process of production. They apply labor power to raw materials to produce commodities, which are appropriated by capitalists. As commodities are exchanged for money, surplus value is realized as profit, and then re-invested as new capital. This is the core of capital, the material manifestation of its existence and expansion. It is what allows capital to reproduce itself.

Some delineate this class more broadly, as all those who own nothing except their ability to work, which they must sell to capitalists in order to survive. But not every working person, laborer, employee or wage-earner is a member of the working class. What defines this class is that their labor power is used by capitalists to produce surplus value.

The production of surplus value is the criteria that makes labor power "productive."

They include:

- Industrial workers, skilled and unskilled
- Construction workers
- Agricultural workers
- Workers involved in resource extraction such as miners and loggers
- Many unemployed workers who are still seeking work (Though not currently productive, they have the potential to be. The reason that there is never full employment under capitalism is because this "reserve army" of the unemployed is required to keep the wages of others down — "If you don't like your pay/conditions/job, there are plenty of others who will take it.")

Petit bourgeoisie (literally "little bourgeoisie"):

This class includes people who may own some form of capital on a small or individual level — not enough to generate more capital (and thus be a capitalist), but enough to keep themselves going. This can be physical capital, such as a shop, or intellectual capital, such as a degree in engineering. These forms of personal capital require some investment and enhance their earning ability. The upper strata of this class aspire to belong to the bourgeoisie, and they identify ideologically with that class.

The petit bourgeoisie also includes service employees, who are "non-productive" laborers/working people (this is not a judgment about the utility of the service or work they perform — it means that their labor power does not generate surplus value, but instead assists in the circulation of capital). Service employees have no access to any means of production, and are often heavily dominated in the exchange of their services for wages. This tends to bring them closer, ideologically, to the working class.

The petit bourgeoisie is not an autonomous class. Because the fundamental conflict in capitalism is between the bourgeoisie and working class, the various strata of the petit bourgeoisie exist in the camp of either of these two fundamental classes. Their interests, along with their loyalties, will mainly tend to attach to whichever of the two fundamental classes is currently dominant (under capitalism, that is the bourgeoisie). This is the case with even the most discontented and radicalized sections of the petit bourgeoisie, who may resist the effects of capitalism (even fiercely), but are not able to fundamentally challenge its existence.

This wide-ranging class includes:

- Small entrepreneurs and business owners
- Skilled professionals such as doctors, lawyers, engineers, programmers, baseball players
- Intellectuals such as artists, writers and academics
- Teachers, journalists, firefighters, police, social workers, bus drivers
- Family farmers
- Small-time drug dealers
- White collar (clerical) employees such as office assistants, telemarketers, cube farm data jockeys
- Service workers including sales clerks, sex workers, health care, and hotel workers

Lumpen:

Lumpen (from "rouge" in German) are those who have no relationship to the social productive process, as well as no independent means of subsistence. They can have roots in or identify with either the proletariat or bourgeoisie, but are de-classed.

Those in the lumpenproletariat are people who have no access to capital, and for whatever reason, cannot or do not want to sell labor power. They may become dependent on the state, friends and family, or charity, or meet their needs through petty theft, panhandling, or some combination of dumpster-diving and couch-surfing.

Those in the lumpenbourgeoisie are people who have access to large amounts of capital, but instead of reinvesting any of it (as a capitalist would), they consume it all. These can be the adult children of capitalists, who live off their parents or trust funds. They may also acquire their wealth through embezzlement, corruption, and other forms of extra-legal thievery (not to be confused with the bureaucratic bourgeoisie, who use their positions within the state apparatus to engage in these types of practices and then invest their ill-gotten gains in capitalist enterprises).

Outside class society:

People who meet their own needs independently without being integrated into the global economy, such as hunter/foragers. Their existence, which requires access to land that remains free of any private control or ownership, is constantly threatened and attacked.

The bourgeois brain

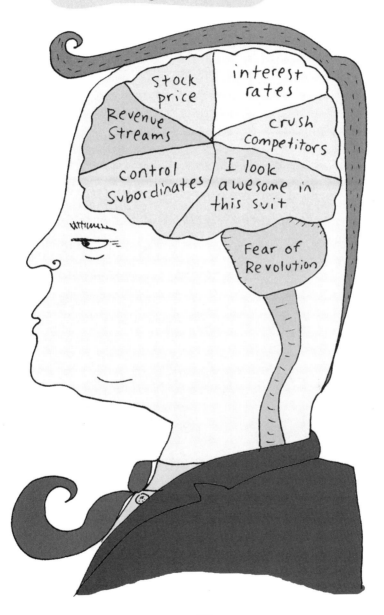

THE VICIOUS ECONOMIC CYCLE

The march of commodities from earth to assembly line to land fill is the basis of, and is represented by, the circulation and accumulation of a very abstract form of wealth, which is money.

Capitalism is, on the one hand, a social relation of domination. It is also an economic process—the endless flow of money to commodity production for the generation of more money.

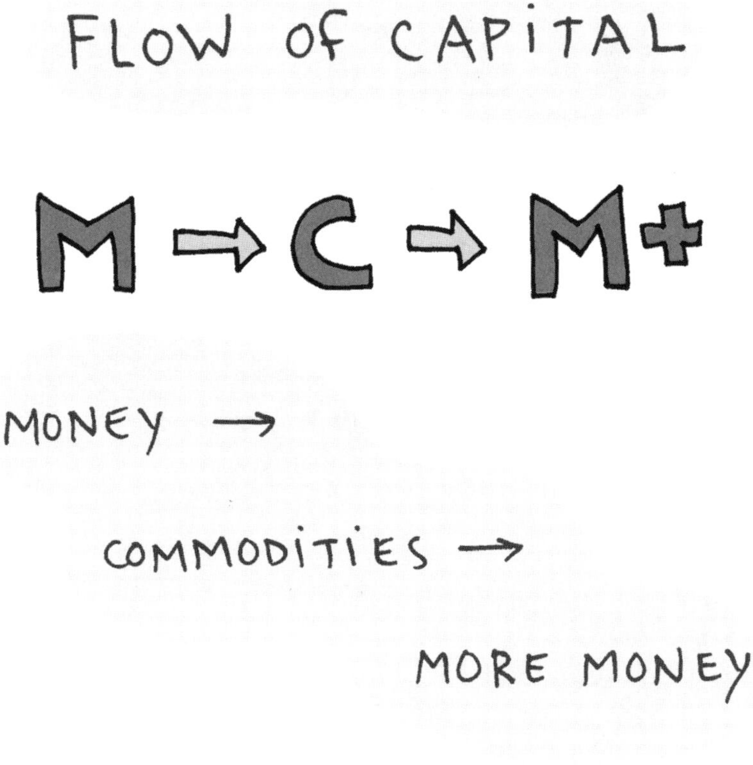

FLOW OF CAPITAL

$$M \Rightarrow C \Rightarrow M+$$

MONEY →

COMMODITIES →

MORE MONEY

But it's not linear; it's both cyclical and progressive, like a spiral.

Here's a simple representation of the process and its major nodal points:

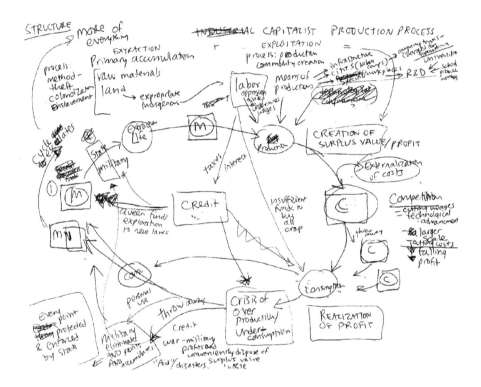

Got that?

I'm kidding! Actually it's way more complicated than this.

Here's an extremely simplified, and necessarily incomplete representation of capitalism's basic economic structure. Since this is a cycle—the ultimate vicious cycle—we can start at any point.

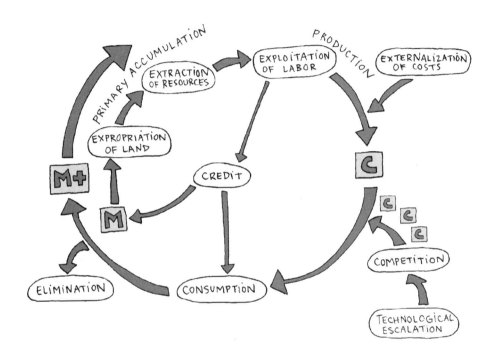

(Since this diagram is really too small if squished onto a single page, and turning it on its side doesn't seem like an elegant option, a larger version is also included, spread across the next two pages with the center overlapping, for easy reference during all the steps outlined in this chapter).

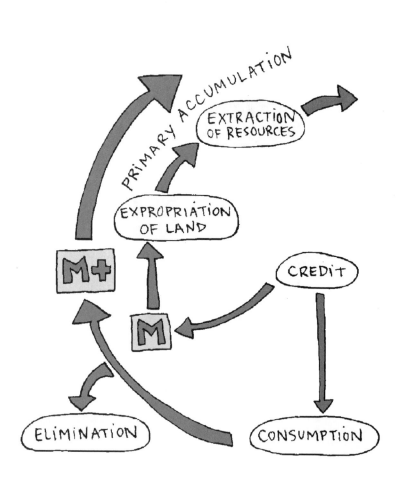

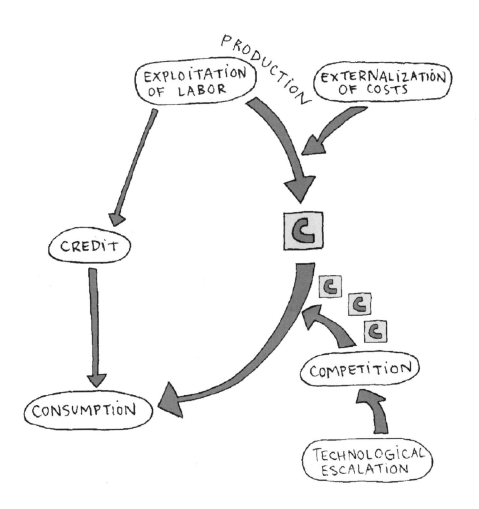

Let's start with what the capitalist starts with: money to invest (M).

A bank or a queen or anyone who already has accumulated surplus wealth extends a line of credit to some explorer to gather a group of armed thugs, go out into the world, locate wealth and steal it.

This first part of the process consists of the expropriation of land and extraction of natural resources. This is also called original, primitive or primary accumulation.

We are sometimes told that this was a practice confined to the colonial period, but it's ongoing. One of today's "great investment opportunities" for imperialists is land-grabbing in Africa, Asia and Latin America for export-oriented mechanized monoculture agribusiness (which entails the violent displacing of subsistence farmers and pastoralists).

The World Bank provides capital for multinational land investors and speculators, who, from 2001-2010, have already taken 203 million hectares (501 million acres) of land. World Bank loans to the agribusiness sector totaled $6-$8 billion in 2012. 56-63% of all arable land in Cambodia has been sold to private investors. More than 30% of land in Liberia has been sold off. As of 2012, 5% of the entire continent of Africa's agricultural land has been sold or leased to foreign investors. In the meantime, 21 formal complaints have been brought against the World Bank by communities whose land rights have been violated.[3]

---

[3] *Our Land, Our Lives: Time Out on the Global Land Rush*, Oxfam Briefing Note, October 2012.

There are many ways that imperialists accomplish the expropriation of land, including overt war, and more subtle means like grain dumping (selling it at prices below production costs) to destroy subsistence farmers. This theft accomplishes a few things in favor of capital. The conqueror can use that land and extract whatever is in it and on it. And as the people are dispossessed — no longer able to live on the land — they are compelled to move to cities and become dependent on jobs. This is how the working class is created and continuously resupplied. It also creates the consumer: without land, we have to buy food, shelter, and all the other things we need.

You will do all the work while I collect the money.
When do I start?

The next part—the key part—of the cycle is production.

The defining features of capitalism are right here at the point of production: the exploitation of labor in the conversion of natural materials into commodities that embody surplus value.

We'll return to that shortly, to describe the process in more detail. It's important enough to require its own section.

Meanwhile, another way that the capitalists add value to their products is through the externalization of costs. Basically, they're not paying the full production costs for the commodities. Pollution from the production process is discharged into the environment. The numerous and serious consequences of this, never mind the cleanup which never happens, are not paid for by the capitalist who caused the problem, but by us, by society as a whole, and by all the living beings on Earth who are affected.

In fact, none of the world's industrial sectors that are in the top 20 (regarding worst environmental impact) would be profitable (*at all!*) if they didn't externalize costs.[4]

[4] *Natural Capital at Risk: The Top 100 Externalities of Business*, report by Trucost, April 15, 2013.

You already have thirty-seven of those.
But not the pink one.
Ka-ching!
27.30
Thank you!
BIG BLOW-OUT SALE

Other capitalists are running this same cycle at the same time. All their commodities flow into the marketplace. Competition is a major economic driving force of capitalism.

Capitalists compete against each other for the sale — by out-marketing each other or by undercutting each other in price. Usually both. This puts pressure on the rate of profit to fall. To remain competitive, the capitalists are forced to continuously cut the costs of production.

Wages are the largest variable cost in most businesses, so there's tremendous pressure on capitalists to keep them as low as possible. To accomplish this, even during periods of high employment they manipulate the economy to keep the unemployment rate at about 5% or higher, so there are always plenty of desperate people competing for jobs.

They move their factories to countries where wages are the lowest they can find, and where repressive governments prevent workers from organizing. (If the governments aren't repressive enough, that will be quickly taken care of).

They pressure laborers to work longer days, and they escalate productivity so that each worker produces ever more surplus value per hour.

Competition drives technological development as each capital-ist pursues ever-increasing efficiency and speed. They mechanize their factories to minimize the number of workers and to stay ahead of one another.

58

Smaller companies that can't keep up are driven out of business or bought up by larger ones, forming monopolies in certain sectors. Four companies control 90% of the world's grain production. Four airlines hold 80% of the market share in the US. eBay controls 90% of the online auction market in the U.S. and Europe. 33% of all laptops in the world are produced by one company (Quanta Computer in Taiwan).

A single firm, AB InBev, produces nearly 25% of the world's beer (more than 200 brands). U.S. company Anheuser-Busch was acquired in 2008 by InBev, which was a merger of Interbrew (which was a merger of Belgian companies Artois and Piedboeuf), and AmBev (which was a merger of Brazilian firms Antarctica and Brahma). Along the way, InBev also picked up Labatt (Canada), Fujian Sedrin (third largest brewery in the world's largest beer market), and several Latin American firms.

Anhueser-Busch even on its own was infamous for its public threats to lower its prices below any other company that attempted to undercut them. This was a very effective tactic to keep beer prices elevated overall.

Market power paves the way for monopolies to employ various means to control prices, to counteract the tendency of the rate of profit to fall. So while the local hardware store is failing, large oil companies (and beer monopolies) are making more money than ever.

The surplus value created in production is locked inside the commodity until the moment of consumption, when it's released as profit.

When you plunk your dollars down to buy the hair dryer or the box of frozen waffles, the capitalist's goal is realized.

Now we run into one of capitalism's major contradictions. In order to make a profit, capitalists must *exploit* workers, in other words, pay them less than the value of the commodities that they produce. So, there will always be more total value on the market than what can be paid for (and consumed) by the domestic population. When markets become saturated, this causes what's called the crisis of over-production. There's too much stuff, and the people will never—can never—be paid enough to buy it all.

(Please read the above paragraph again; it contains the clearest explanation of why perpetual economic growth under capitalism is a non-negotiable imperative, no matter how destructive—and thus why the system can't be reformed and must be crushed).

The goal of each individual capitalist is to maximize profits, in other words, to accumulate as much surplus value as possible, to reinvest as new capital. But for the system overall, too much surplus value causes problems. It can't all be absorbed back into the economy.

What do they do with it? They can't just leave it lying around to depreciate; they have to put it to work somehow.

The REALIZATION of SURPLUS VALUE

It's just a damn hair dryer.

irrational growth

A portion of surplus value is siphoned off for personal use by capitalists, to furnish extravagant lifestyles with excessive salaries and bonuses.

Some surplus value is simply thrown away, eliminated through waste, wars (more than 54% of the US discretionary budget is spent on perpetrating violent imperialist world domination, terrorizing and killing millions of people in the process), and so-called international "aid" (which is also employed to extend and intensify imperialist domination). The latter two also function as centers for creating even more profit, which they are compelled to pursue, but which also exacerbates the overall problem.

They desperately ramp up the level of consumption with infusions of credit, basing the consumer economy on debt. They issue loans like crazy, even while knowing they can't possibly ever all be paid off. Of course this creates bubbles and instability, which grow progressively worse.

They must continuously force open and seize control of more markets. This is one of the driving forces for imperialism. When more than one country does this, major inter-imperialist conflicts ensue. This rivalry — not any sort of moral issue — was the cause of the two major inter-imperialist wars (the so-called "world wars") of the 20th Century. So imperialist war both captures markets and destroys excess product — it's capitalist multitasking.

Back at the start of the economic cycle, the surplus value has to be reinvested. Only through expansion can each company gain a competitive edge over all the others. For capitalism as a whole to function in a reasonably stable way, for capital investment (especially in heavy industry) to be worthwhile and for everyone to stay ahead of their interest payments, it must grow at least about 3% annually.

So the cycle goes around again, but bigger. In the next turn, they must extract more raw materials, exploit more labor, manufacture more products, generate more waste, make more profits. Growth is not just linear, because each turn of the cycle is on top of a greater quantity than the time before.

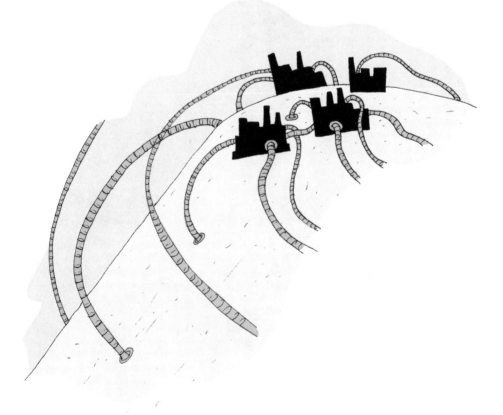

Continuous growth isn't easy. We see economists and politicians on the news all the time trying to figure out how to keep it going. But as economies become saturated, there's less opportunity for profitable investment. So they have to invent ways to turn more things into profit generators, invading us through privatization and assigning monetary value to every aspect of our lives, from our emotions to genetic material.

THE COMMODITY

So, now we'll define what a commodity is, and examine how surplus value is produced.

Here, on the next page, we have the commodity. (The yellow rectangle. Go with it).

The capitalist has already acquired the means of production (a factory, machinery, materials and so on) through previous cycles of expropriation/dispossession (recall the earlier explorer and entourage of thugs), extraction, unequal trading, and exploitation.

Primitive accumulation continues to be the way raw materials are acquired. Basically this means capitalists or their proxies invade, tear up the land (disregarding the effects on whoever's already living there), and abscond with whatever can be turned into something to sell. If it's not a group of thugs armed with guns, then they're armed with laws, money, or other persuasive extortion techniques.

Capitalism's early form was mercantilism, a method of accumulating profit through unequal trades. This became start-up capital for the development of industry.

The capitalist in our current example already possesses the means of production, which is the congealed surplus value from previous cycles of exploitation, continuously becoming available to be reinvested as capital.

COMMODITY

Pretend this is a commodity. The thing you covet.

It's a rectangle. Who wants a rectangle? I'd rather have a carrot.

It's an abstract representation. For a diagram. Use your imagination.

I'll imagine I'm at the beach.

COMMODITY fig. 2

THE CAPITALIST CONTRIBUTES
THE RAW MATERIALS AND
MEANS OF PRODUCTION.

74

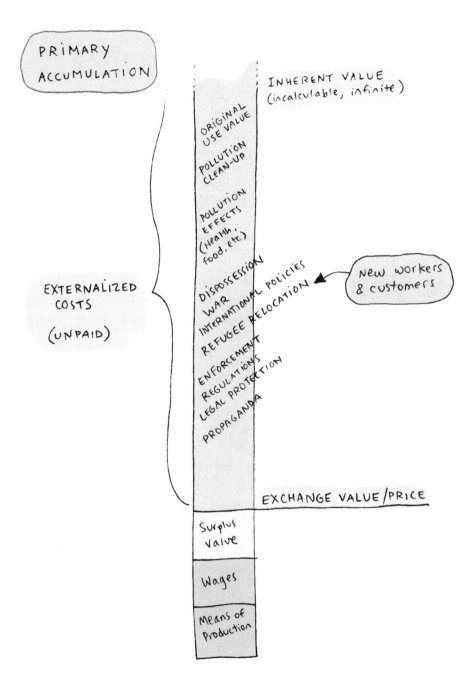

PRIMARY
ACCUMULATION

INHERENT VALUE
(incalculable, infinite)

ORIGINAL USE VALUE

POLLUTION CLEAN-UP

POLLUTION EFFECTS (Health, food, etc)

DISPOSSESSION

WAR

INTERNATIONAL POLICIES

REFUGEE RELOCATION

ENFORCEMENT

REGULATIONS

LEGAL PROTECTION

PROPAGANDA

New workers & customers

EXTERNALIZED COSTS

(UNPAID)

EXCHANGE VALUE/PRICE

Surplus Value

Wages

Means of Production

COMMODITY fig. 3

THE WORKER IS PAID
ONLY ENOUGH TO
SURVIVE AND REPRODUCE.
THE REST OF THE DAY,
S/HE WORKS FOR FREE.

Keep going.
And make
it snappy.

UNPAID
LABOR
POWER
(SURPLUS
VALUE)

PAID
LABOR
POWER
(WAGE
LABOR)

MEANS
OF
PRODUCTION

RAW
MATERIALS

The worker, who possesses or controls no means of production, must sell her or his labor power to the capitalist. This labor power, which will be used to produce commodities for the capitalist, is itself sold as a commodity. The price (paid as wages) is not based on the value of the commodities it will be used to produce (it is completely unrelated to that, actually), but roughly on the cost of its *own* production: the worker's subsistence and reproduction, the replenishment of the class. But because of heavy capitalist and/or imperialist domination, workers are often compelled to accept sub-survival wages.

During the working day, the worker produces more value than the amount of wages they receive. The labor power that produces that extra value is not paid for. It is surplus value.

In our example, let's pretend that wages are $50 a day, and that the other costs associated with production—the materials and the depreciation of machinery, rent for the factory and other inputs—are also $50 per day, which adds up to $100 of total costs.

The capitalist puts the labor power to work. Let's say each worker produces goods worth (that have an average exchange value of) $50 every hour. That means the costs associated with production—$100 of wages and inputs—are covered within 2 hours. Then the rest of the day, whatever the worker produces is surplus value. If the working day is 8 hours, the surplus value will be $300. The value of the product is all that put together: $400.

The fact that the capitalist owns the means of production is used to justify that the worker has no legal right to keep the product; so the capitalist takes everything that the worker produces. The amount of wages and of surplus value is contested, determined by class struggle in all fields of social relations (economic, ideological, and political).

COMMODITY fig. 4

The capitalist then sells the product at its value. The surplus value is already in the product, generated in the process of production itself. It's realized at the point of sale, as profit. If it's bought by a retailer, an additional amount is added on to the final retail price. This is not additional surplus value, but instead is the imposition of an unequal exchange between the merchant and the customer. The customer is paying more than the actual value of the commodity, because of the greater market power of the retailer.

If the retailer is a monopoly, it can use its market power to dominate capitalists, to set its purchase price below the actual value of the commodity. This is one manifestation of imperialism, a way that surplus value is extracted from dominated countries. This puts pressure on the capitalist, who in turn intensifies pressure on the workers. Often, their wages are pushed extremely low, barely more than nothing.

COMMODITY fig.5

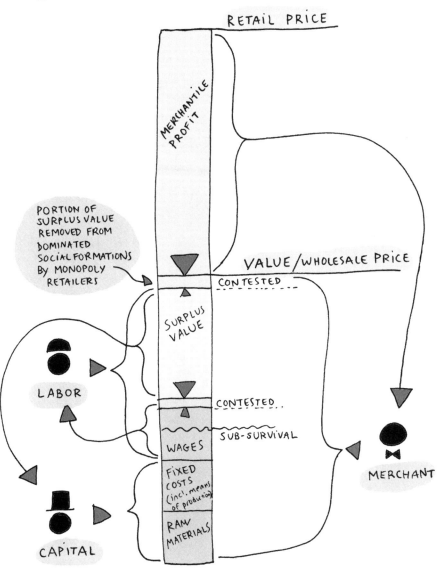

RETAIL PRICE

MERCHANTILE PROFIT

PORTION OF SURPLUS VALUE REMOVED FROM DOMINATED SOCIAL FORMATIONS BY MONOPOLY RETAILERS

VALUE/WHOLESALE PRICE

CONTESTED

SURPLUS VALUE

LABOR

CONTESTED

SUB-SURVIVAL

WAGES

FIXED COSTS (incl. means of production)

RAW MATERIALS

CAPITAL

MERCHANT

We see this practice of super-exploitation being perpetrated by giant multinational retailers such as Walmart and Gildan.

GILDAN, A CANADIAN APPAREL COMPANY, HAS FACTORIES AROUND THE WORLD, AND CLAIMS TO BE "SOCIALLY RESPONSIBLE."

WHY IS CAPITALISM
SO DESTRUCTIVE?

The problem is not the greed of individual capitalists (though they are greedy). It's structural. Capitalists are merely social agents who fill positions that are required and generated by capital as it reproduces itself. Capital has motion, necessities, a life of its own. Capitalists, the stewards or servants of capital, are compelled to maximize surplus value by whatever means necessary.

Capitalism is currently facing a convergence of crises: of overproduction, financial instability, and ecological catastrophe. Yet they can't ease up on production, but continue to forge ahead. It reaches such irrational proportions that in China, there are 12-24 massive cities built each year that have no people living in them.[5] At the same time, not coincidentally, 80% of that country's rivers no longer support aquatic life.

Industrial/extractive expansion is causing global, terminal ecological crisis. We already have radioactive rain, methane plumes, runaway wildfires, superstorms, rising seas, shrimp without eyes, and tap water that can be lit on fire. If unchecked, pollution, water shortages, nuclear radiation, soil depletion, global warming and geo-engineering could wipe out all life on Earth. But the internal structural economic crises are, for capitalists, even more urgent than the ecological crisis. The ecological crisis is simply collateral damage, an effect or consequence of their main pursuit. The capitalist growth imperative cannot be denied.

[5] *China's Real Estate Bubble*, 60 Minutes, March 3, 2013.

It seems obvious, but few admit: you can't have infinite growth on a finite planet.

Today the crisis of overproduction has become acute and the system is maxed out. It's reaching the end of all physical limits. Capitalists are desperate to find profitable places to invest their money, which is rapidly accumulating with nowhere to go. In 2010, David Bianco, the head of U.S. equity strategy at Bank of America, said: "Cash is piling up faster than companies can figure out what to do with it."

In 2011, US corporations were sitting on $1.6 trillion in cash. Tycoons like Warren Buffett and Bill Gates expressed the desire to be taxed, and dumped billions of dollars into charitable foundations. Of course philanthropy generates big profits, so the system ends up further saturated, but it also opens up additional investment opportunities.

Oh, you thought the purpose of philanthropy was to help people...? How cute.

Extremist, destructive industrial practices are quickly becoming their only options, like railway expansion to transport tar sands oil to Texas refineries, fracking for natural gas even when it contaminates groundwater and causes methane-spewing earthquakes, strong-arming the entire world into accepting genetically modified foods, and expanding nuclear power plants with no clue about where they're going to store the radioactive waste.

It might be tempting to hope that capitalism will collapse on its own. Unfortunately, the system isn't going to smash itself. Capitalism in crisis becomes even more ruthless. They no longer even bother to keep up the pretense of caring about the future.

Resource depletion and natural disasters aren't problems for capitalists — in fact, scarcity makes prices and profits soar, and catastrophes are huge investment opportunities. The only panic that a capitalist feels when contemplating the melting of the Arctic is that he won't get to the newly uncovered oil first. They don't care where they get their energy, as long as they control it all. The system is dynamic, adaptable, and infinitely ruthless.

Capitalism will ultimately destroy itself, but only when it's destroyed all life on the planet, which is too late to matter. Until then, capitalism is all about breaking through limitations. That's what it always does.

There is no escape from our need to crush it now, while we still have a living planet to save.

AN IMAGINARY
ECONOMY

Capital, having saturated the globe, has expanded beyond physical limits. Increasingly, capitalists have been busting through the over-production problem by bypassing the production process altogether. As industrial production has surpassed the capacity of world markets to purchase and consume its products, the pressure of too much capital to invest has forced governments to relax regulations and allow more fictitious value into their national economies, leading to the current global dominance of the financial/investment sector.

There has been increasing conflict within the capitalist class over the character of current and future growth: concrete surplus value extracted from labor power on the one hand ("working capital"), vs., on the other hand, inflated forms that are increasingly unstable ("ficticious capital"). Money makes more money (but no material value) through debt, deficits, speculation, arbitrage, and by simply printing more of it.

FINANCE CAPITAL

$$M \Rightarrow M+$$

MONEY →

COMMITIES →

MORE MONEY

THE SHIFT OF CAPITAL FROM INDUSTRY TO FINANCE

This seems to throw production—along with workers and consumers—out of the equation. They don't appear to need us so much any more. This is reflected in our high unemployment rate and falling incomes.

In the US, mainly due to automation, six million US manufacturing jobs vanished between the years 2000 and 2011. Also, the relative proportion of finance capitalism in the US economy has increased. From the mid-1940s until the early 1980s, about half of all corporate profits were obtained through manufacturing, and less than 15% through finance. By 2007 the US financial sector had grown to 1.8 times the size of the manufacturing sector.[6]

Still, the industrial output of the US has not declined in total, though it has fallen relative not only to finance but also to other countries, which are growing at a faster rate. A decade ago, US manufacturing was the largest in the world, four times greater than China's; today the US has slipped into second place after China. In 1970, the U.S. produced 29% of the world's commodities; by 2009 it stood at 18%.[7]

Commodity production is still the largest part of the global economy, but finance has risen more rapidly, increasing its proportion relative to industry. In 1978, 2% of global profit came from finance. By 2011 it increased to 42%.[8] So the rising influence of finance capital on the economy is considerable, and it's destabilizing. But producing more commodities is destabilizing too.

[6] p. 51, *Beware of Capitalist Sharks,* Richard Greeman, Praxis Research and Education Center, 2012.

[7] *Manufacturing Output By Country,* Greyhill Advisors, 2011; citing United Nations Conference on Trade and Development, 2009.

[8] *A Definition of Imperialism,* Abdy Javadzadeh, presentation for One Struggle, Florida International University, 2011.

Capital's escape from production and ability to find refuge in the ballooning financial industry is merely relative, partial and temporary. It's not a long-term solution for the crisis of over-production, but merely prolongs the agony.

The massive amounts of money pouring into stocks, commodity markets, bonds, credit, currencies, real estate, and other instruments of speculation (at least not tulips this time) causes great instability as the amount of fictitious value in the economy increases. As gamblers (sorry, investors) begin to acknowledge that their holdings are artificially inflated, that there's nothing underpinning them but bad debt and toxic assets, the bubbles inevitably crash. Financial crises occur as these worthless assets are dumped en masse. After prices collapse, the risks once again become attractive and buying begins anew.

Each turn of the cycle generates more fear and greed than the one before.

Financial collapse has happened many times before, and it will again. It causes chaos and shakeups. Business interests large and small fail, increasing the suffering of the majority of people who are trapped inside and dependent on the economy.

For the sector of the capitalist class that favors the lower risks (though lower returns) of industry, a catastrophic financial crisis could be an opportunity to restructure the system in its favor, weaken the hegemony of finance capital, and strengthen the role of manufacturing.

An economic "reset" to a lower level could spark a new round of the accumulation process, based more solidly on the production of material commodities that contain real surplus value, on which their entire economy ultimately rests.

Growth based on real, concrete value can fundamentally only be achieved by constantly increasing the rate of exploitation (the extraction of surplus value from the working class). To this end, industrial capital is using financial crisis, high unemployment, inflated food and energy prices, and global "structural adjustment" (austerity) measures, to put tremendous pressure on an increasingly desperate working class. Their aim is to force workers to accept the sub-survival wages and atrocious working conditions that come with these industrial jobs.

Factoring in the costs of transporting goods, the wages of workers in China and the US are moving toward parity. We are already seeing some gestures toward a resurgence of domestic production in the US, but re-set at a lower level. These won't be union jobs allowing decent living conditions, and forget getting enough work hours to qualify for health care. Watch for more "right to work" states, and even US free trade zones and the elimination of the minimum wage. They'll tell us these are unfortunate-but-necessary temporary measures to "help" us through tough times.

Meanwhile, governments attempt to regulate and stabilize the spiraling global economic crisis by doing everything possible to stimulate economic growth of any kind.

This is extremely difficult and complex. The crisis of faith in the financial sector impacts industry too, because the two forms of capital have become so intertwined. When one receives medicine, the other suffers side effects. Industry has come to depend on credit at every step: to capitalize itself, to operate, and to facilitate the consumption of goods. Plus they've become extremely dependent on the inflation of the speculative value of their companies — their stock price.

Cycles are becoming more volatile: credit dries up, then pressure builds until it must be released again into the economy, but these measures must be ever more extreme (such as central banks dropping interest rates to near 0%), which undermine the system overall even more.

As industrial capital declines relatively in power, and the financial sector experiences ever-more volatile boom-and-crash cycles that reverberate through the global economy, banks have fewer options they can exercise in response, because they've already implemented whatever they can do to facilitate growth (they can't go below 0% interest rates). These current forms of capital are reaching their ultimate limits.

MARCHING TOWARD FASCISM

To deal with their economic dilemna, capital has begun to be increasingly diverted into private/state hybrid enterprises.

This is a way to force more commodities into the economy and to increase production for its own sake (for immediate destruction rather than for use). These enterprises include wars, foreign so-called "aid," geo-engineering, disaster response, and government subsidies.

In addition, there is an increasing flow of public funds to private hands through the privatization of public institutions (prisons, detention centers, schools, military, medical facilities), and the creation of ever-more toxic new "needs" (such as pollution creating the need for more health care and insurance). As public social services are cut under austerity programs, public/private "partnerships" in the form of NGOs are proliferating. (By recruiting sincere progressives, these also serve to co-opt opposition. Capitalists are, once again, extremely good at multi-tasking!)

The state will mandate and/or partly fund the masses' increased involuntary consumption of all of these—through our taxes, through legislation such as Obamacare, and through increased numbers of people being forced into institutions of various types.

As capital puts increasing pressure on wages while profiting off the warehousing of populations, the working class will be pushed into virtual slavery through prison labor and work-for-food arrangements (both of which are on the increase worldwide).

State control over production and over the allocation of resources, in conjunction with privately appropriated profit, plus the socialization of losses, is an economic aspect of fascism. Slave labor is another aspect.

This trend is still emerging but is gaining strength. It is being attacked by some sections of capitalists for now; while at the same time they are competing to enter it, and are pushing for its expansion in order to ease their own entry into it. They recognize it as one of their only options of survival as capitalists.

There is an intensifying contradiction in the economy overall between short-term and long-term viability, and there's a need for a major shift in how capital reproduces itself. In the current conjuncture, capitalism must destroy toxic value and restructure the whole economy. In this painful transition, their long-term needs as a class clash with their immediate imperatives as individual competing capitals/blocs. Some will not go along with this voluntarily.

The internal class conflict between industrial and financial sectors will likely continue to intensify. It may even break out into civil war, pressing a divided population to fight for the different fractions of the class that dominates them.

Obama is doing his best to manage the immediate conflicting needs of different blocs of capital as he implements policies that lay the basis for the long-term viability of the system—putting in place the political and economic structures for fascism and facilitating the transition of capital investments into alignment with it.

The fact that he's a Democrat encourages the compliance of the masses, directing their demands into channels that will benefit capital as a whole and closing off all other options. Until a real alternative becomes available, they're trapped between politicians who pay lip service to their needs while crushing them, and others who openly don't care about them at all.

It may seem irrational that capitalists can't work together to solve their common problems without all the drama and crisis.

Instead of converting the last remnants of the natural world into junk, killing not only us but also themselves and their own children in the process, why can't they invest their extra wealth in positive projects such as land rehabilitation? Instead of going to war with themselves over the best way to accumulate profit, why not meet the people's basic needs so they don't revolt?

Capitalism seems to make no sense when you look at it as a non-capitalist. Yet it has its own internal logic because individual capitalists are driven by competition. Their gain is someone else's loss, and vice-versa. They face tremendous, relentless pressure to choose immediate short-term profits even over their own long-term survival. For them, it is each against all.

They can cooperate to a certain degree, and they do (especially when it comes to repressing, pacifying and disorganizing the rest of us), but the relationship between them is essentially antagonistic. Competition is their default setting. When forced to deflect immediate catastrophes, they do manage to act collectively through the political representatives of the particular sections of their class (Republicans and Democrats), and through the state as a whole, which represents their class as a whole. A recent example is their raising the debt ceiling barely in time to remain solvent another day.

Because each capitalist must protect its own bottom line above all other concerns, each one is in a permanent mode of vicious rivalry against all the others. They are incapable of sacrificing short-term gain for long-term benefit, even to save themselves.

Their decisions are not based on what's good or rational, they're based on what makes the most money at that moment. What will make the most profit in the least amount of time? This, and only this, is what they are driven to do. They really have no choice. The individuals can't decide on their own that they're going to change that system, or even behave in a slightly less evil manner, because their competitors will push any advantage and drive them out of business.

Capitalists are driven by a blind imperative to pursue the most accessible and immediate and highest possible profits, no matter how irrationally they're obtained, and regardless of their personal desires. They can't care whether or not what's produced is useful or good. For destroying the environment to maximize profits, executives get promoted. For changing their policies out of concern for the environment or the well-being of people, and consequently making less profit, they'd be instantly replaced.

IN QUIET MOMENTS OF REFLECTION, THE CAPITALIST SEARCHES HIS SOUL, THE DEPTHS OF HIS TRUE BEING, FOR ANSWERS TO THE ESSENTIAL QUESTIONS OF LIFE AND MEANING.

CLASS INTERESTS DETERMINE OUR IDEAS.

OBJECTIVE REALITY

SUBJECTIVE INTERPRETATION

GUNS, TELEVISION, AND OTHER FORMS OF PERSUASION

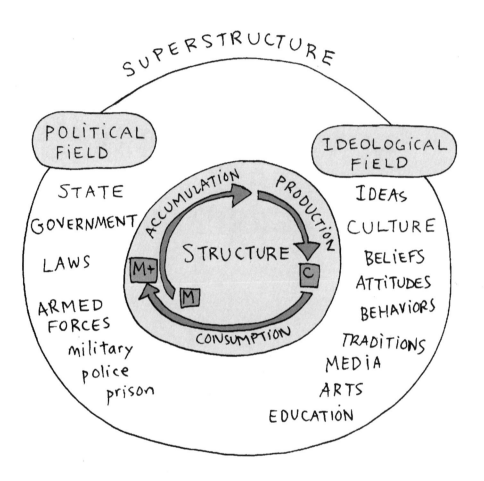

You may wonder why anyone would put up with this miserable nightmare for even one second. We do because of the superstructure — the ideas (or ideology) and political institutions that we can picture as a shell around the economic structure, both supporting it and shaped by its needs.

The superstructure is made up of the political and the ideological fields.

The political field:

The sole purpose of the state is to keep the flow of capital running smoothly.

It administers and regulates the process with its government and legal system.

It regulates both the relations within a single class, and between different classes.

It enforces the dominance of the capitalist class with its military, police, prison complex, and security apparatus.

The ideological field:

The prevailing ideology of any society serves the interests of its dominant class. The only ideas allowed to participate in the capitalist marketplace are pro-system; any others are either actively suppressed or starved of support. The dominant culture tells us how to think and behave through the stories and myths of mainstream media, entertainment, and religion.

It indoctrinates us in its schools.

Its traditions train us in habits of individualism, competition, and subservience to authority.

Its ideologies reinforce structural oppression to divide the working class, such as misogyny, racism, homophobia, xenophobia and nationalism.

The nuclear family is a self-policing social unit enforcing the domination of children and women, a personal mini-state right inside our own homes.

Is this all there is?

You can't live without me, commerce asserts—I feed you. Competition is natural, says science. Shut up and obey, snarls Homeland Security. Don't complain, says your supervisor. Advertising reassures us that the latest pill or consumer item will numb our pain. The talking heads of corporate media decide for us what matters and what doesn't. The entire weight of this culture whispers without pause into our ears: "The way things are will always be."

The multitudinous voices for the status quo jabber so relentlessly that we start to believe that they're coming from inside our own heads. Not only do we refrain from taking action; many of us even dissuade others from doing so.

How often have you heard the following?

- There's no point.
- You can't win.
- They'll fire you or kill you if you speak up.
- You'll end up unemployed, in prison, or dead, for nothing.
- The enemy is too powerful.
- No one else will join you.
- There will always be inequality and injustice.
- Human nature is greedy.
- Just take care of yourself and your family. Grow up.
- Nothing will change.
- It's not worth it.

Are these arguments true? At least partly—that's why they're so convincing. Social transformation is indeed difficult. It's a long shot, with an uncertain outcome. It requires determination, risk, and sacrifice.

However, they're also partly not true.

Many well-intentioned people justify inaction by allowing themselves to be convinced that nothing can be done. But if they were honest, they would admit that even if something could be done, they still wouldn't stick their necks out. Especially if the results aren't guaranteed. They believe that to act, and possibly (or probably) fail, is not worth risking whatever level of security (no matter how tenuous) they currently possess.

Heartless as that calculation may seem, it's not wholly irrational. Why would you throw yourself at the machine and possibly lose your freedom, or even your life, and make your family suffer, if it has only a slight chance of accomplishing anything?

Really, why would you? Why does anyone?

Because there is that chance. And we want to, need to, take it.

If we don't, the alternative will be unbearable, unlivable.

Without people willing to stick their necks out, the United States would still have slavery. Women wouldn't be allowed to vote. The fourteen-hour workday would be the norm. The United States military would still be killing people across the world—oh wait...

Nothing changes, until people decide to make them change. Until *we* decide to make them change, to act even if the odds are against us.

Silence those cynical, hopeless, enemy voices. Raise our own.

We need to break through this superstructure to smash the economic core of capital. We have to stop the production of surplus value, which is what allows capitalism to reproduce itself.

PART 2:
WHAT IS TO BE DONE NOW?

How to smash capitalism?

If it was easy, we'd have done it a thousand times already. There is no magic formula, no "The Answer." But there is a rich history of experience, previous attempts resulting in advances and setbacks, from which we can learn lessons and draw certain principles.

If we want to emancipate ourselves from this omnicidal nightmare, then we must organize ourselves, must become strong enough so that we can both defeat capital and offer an alternative.

Only through collective struggle can we dispossess the dispossessors, take back our collective means of subsistence, and defeat capitalism as a system. As a result of that process, we can begin to build a way of life that is sustainable and free of class divisions and all forms of domination.

130

EYES ON THE PRIZE: GOAL + STRATEGY + TACTICS = POLITICAL LINE

Begin with the end in mind

The future we get, insofar as we have influence over it, will be shaped by the goals we define today. Our goals in turn determine our strategy. And our tactics, our day-to-day activities, flow from our strategy. We have to get each part of the sequence right—if we err in our aim or trajectory, we'll wind up somewhere we never wanted to go, our efforts all in vain.

We need to develop our capacity to analyze political and social phenomena. Any effective political agent (that's you and me, if we do our work) must develop a political line. It will be more or less correct, or correspondent to reality, depending on our current level of theoretical and ideological maturity.

Our line is our backbone, the foundational structure that determines our struggle as a whole. All our actions are built upon this. A correct line will determine what we understand to be important and what can be ignored, and allows us to creatively and intelligently assess and respond to every situation that arises. Without a correct line, we'll make repeated mistakes and waste our time and energy with a multitude of diversions.

A correct political line doesn't arise spontaneously in anyone's mind, and it can't be absorbed simply by reading political theory (though this certainly helps). It is developed collectively over time and through discussion and practice. It's a never-ending process—there is always more to learn, and deeper levels of understanding to be achieved. It spreads in all directions through exchanges between people: a newly active person has much to teach a seasoned veteran, and vice versa.

A strategy for social transformation can be distilled down to three elements: affirmation (i.e.: spread ideas, prepare minds, raise consciousness, break down ideological domination); consolidation (organize forces); and struggle against the enemy. These basic elements can be endlessly interpreted and elaborated upon, and worked out to the most minute detail.

Decisions must be made: Where to draw the line between you and the enemy? Who is your social base? Who are your allies and how does this shift according to circumstance? What does victory look like? Will possibilities to advance likely emerge mainly from patient preparation and movement building, or through spontaneous responses to conjunctural events, or some combination of these?

Every organization has to work this out for itself, collectively among its members, using lessons from the rich history of our movement, and working backward from the goal.

As for concrete plans, these can only go so far and must constantly be re-evaluated. We can't know precisely what will spark off large-scale resistance or rebellion in any given place. These are always unpredictable, and sometimes don't even make much sense until afterward. Whether they substantially challenge the system or not depends on how prepared (how well-organized) people are to push things beyond the reformist paradigm. What can be done to prepare for these moments that will inevitably occur? This is what we should be concerned with today.

Too many times, out of desperation or impatience to be doing something, people jump into action without a strategy. When people put tactics ahead of strategy, they won't end up where they want to go. They might either end up in jail, useless to the struggle, or they might end up trapped in an endless, ineffectual "protest mode," ambulance chasing, jumping from one campaign to another. When we react to events without a strategy, then when the immediate urgency inevitably dissipates, so do our organizations. We need to build organizations that can withstand the ebb and flow of external events.

Our first priority is to define overall goals. Then we must work backward to develop strategy: how do we get from here to there? Tactics should only be considered after those other elements are clear, and should serve those elements. We shouldn't bother with action for action's sake, but understand how everything we do fits into our overall plan.

Brief definitions:

Goal: The desired objective or result. This should define and guide one's actions. There can be a series of short-term objectives on the way to a relatively final one.

Political line: This is the path from where we are now to where we are going. It corresponds to our interpretation of current reality and the possibilities emerging within it (which adjusts along with the constantly changing reality itself) and determines our practice at all times. We all have a political line and are putting it into practice every day, whether we acknowledge it or not— whether it consists of "keep voting every few years and hope that someone will do something to change things" or "build revolutionary organizations capable of confronting the system." A political line is conveyed by strategy and manifests through tactics.

Strategy, or strategic line: The long-term trajectory of practice, aiming for the ultimate objective.

Tactics, or tactical line: The immediate, concrete practice corresponding to current necessities, situated in the context of the strategy as a whole. Though tactics are determined by strategy, it is through our practice of them that we can constantly evaluate whether or not our strategy is correct, or must be revised.

Priorities: Immediate activities, consciously undertaken in harmony with a political line.

Tactics for what?

There's been a lot of heated debate about "diversity of tactics," particularly since Occupy.

How many blog inches have been devoted to arguing about whether it's wrong or useless or awesome (or varying degrees of okay in different particular circumstances) to break windows at a demonstration? How many conflicts among demonstrators have occurred between those who want to do it and those who want to prevent it from being done?

By itself, the question is useless.

Focusing on tactics misses the point. We can argue with each other for a million years whether property destruction is violence or not, whether voting is violence or not, and whether violence in the abstract is good, bad, or a necessary evil. But it is all empty debate if we avoid the main topic we should be discussing: what's it for?

Action for action's sake is a stupid waste of time and energy. Everything we do should fit into an overall plan. A tactic cannot be judged outside its context. It should be a manifestation of a political line, in harmony with a strategy that has consistency between its short-term and long-term aspects. It should serve a specific goal.

If you argue for a tactic, you should be able to explain how it gets us where we need to go. This shouldn't be vague, but must be worked out as a rational theory. Only with that understanding can the actual employment of that tactic, and its results, be judged as effective (or not).

I respect "diversity of tactics" and everything, but what are you trying to accomplish?
"Accomplish"?

THE FIGHT OF THE ERA: CAPITAL VS. LABOR

Capitalism's fundamental contradiction

All of the history of class-divided society has developed because of class struggle. Class struggle is what moves society forward. Class struggle is the means to transform society.

The fundamental contradiction of capitalism (its defining internal mechanism, what makes it exist, the back-and-forth dynamic that allows it to reproduce itself from day to day) is capital vs. labor. This is manifested in class struggle between capitalists (the bourgeoisie) and workers (the proletariat).

Workers are exploited by capitalists in the process of the production of surplus value.

This economic relationship is embedded in a social relationship, which is one of domination.To force them to produce, and to accept exploitation, capitalists dominate workers not only economically, but also politically and ideologically. The working class resists in all three fields. Class struggle is constant and inherently antagonistic. It can only be resolved by total social transformation, by the end of capitalism.

The fact that capital vs. labor is the fundamental contradiction doesn't mean it's necessarily the most important one—that's a value judgment that will be made differently by people depending on their positions and interests. What it means, instead, is that the push-pull of the struggle between capital and wage-labor is what moves society in the direction it is going. It is the engine driving society over an economic and ecological cliff.

It is only by the workers overturning and destroying this entire ensemble of social relations through which capital reproduces itself, that capitalism can be stopped. When workers emancipate themselves, they emancipate all of society from the domination of capital.

To accomplish this, workers must overturn political domination (smash the state and seize political power through revolution) in order to take the means of production and subsistence out of private hands, and abolish wage labor. Only then can the motive of production be disconnected from the drive to accumulate profit (realized through surplus value).

The struggle against surplus value must be led by those who produce it (who produce all the concrete value in society, in fact): the working class. This is the only class that can follow through to the end, to actually defeat capitalism and offer an alternative. No other class is capable of this.

In line with that orientation, those of us directly exploited by capital have only one way forward: to organize ourselves to crush capitalism. This will require defeating and dismantling the capitalist state, and asserting sufficient power to transform the entire ideological/political/economic structures of society.

For those of us who are not productive (of surplus value) workers but are still part of the popular masses (the natural allies of the working class, who are also dominated and attacked by capitalism), we can weaken capital by struggling for our own interests under the leadership of the working class.

Because capitalism is at a global stage of imperialism, the struggle against it is also global. Capitalists are organized internationally; we must be also. Around the world, we share a common cause and face a common enemy. Wherever we are, we must link together in our fight against both imperialism and capitalism, as well as build solidarity among all the popular classes for these struggles led by the international working class.

What is a revolution?

Imagine that you're in the middle of a furious crowd of people, shaking fists, hoisting signs, screaming for blood. You can't begin to count them — it seems like millions and maybe it is — filling the streets as far as you can see in all directions, in the heart of any major city. They're all fed up with being robbed at every turn by the thugs who run society. They want jobs with decent wages, healthcare, affordable food and housing, and an end to corruption, wars, police state repression and the destruction of the planet. They're demanding dignity, lives worth living. They're willing to fight. They want to win.

Popular rage has been building for a long time, bubbling under the surface, popping up here and there until finally it explodes into a glorious spontaneous uprising that seems to challenge the very heights of the power structure and open up new possibilities for a better world.

Let's assume that in this scenario (just like in real life) we don't have any substantial, well-prepared revolutionary organizations. What is likely to happen?

If the people's mobilization is strong, determined, and persistent, and if increasing social disorder threatens to bring the economy to a halt, then the political party in power may step down.

Yay, victory!
...

Or is it?

Who steps in? The other major party, not significantly different from the first? An organized reactionary or right-wing formation that leads us down a road we haven't bargained for? The military or some fraction thereof?

None of these options would improve things—on the contrary, they'd drag us further along into horrors unknown. But in the absence of an organized and militant alternative political formation, one or another of these miserable options is probably all we're going to get.

What revolutions are not

Transfers of power, by themselves, are not revolutions. Militant mass actions, by themselves, are not revolutions. Uprisings and insurrections—no matter how popular—by themselves, are not revolutions. These may accomplish some positive changes, and they could be steps on a road to revolution. But if we stop there, we have not yet won.

What are we talking about when we use the word "revolution"? Revolution, distilled to its essence, is the ongoing process of the conscious, organized, active exercise of power for the purpose of emancipation.

A genuine revolution requires emancipation of the dominated sections of people, plus the corresponding defeat of the (now former) dominating class—expropriating their holdings and depriving them of the power to rule—and the subsequent fundamental transformation of the entire society, including:

- The ways people meet their material needs
- All social relations
- The prevailing ideas that support those social relations

146

Opportunities for revolution are few and far between. Most people in history live out their lives within a relatively stable social order. Whether they like it or not, there's not much they can do about it. You can't conjure a revolution out of stability any more than you can force an apple to ripen faster on the tree.

But we are living in a special time. Revolutionary conditions are maturing, and we have a decision to make. Do we bite, or let this fruit fall and rot on the ground?

Objective conditions must be ripe

For a revolution to occur, three conditions must exist:

- A ruling class that is crippled by internal conflict, so much so that it can no longer effectively assert its dominance over society.
- A general feeling among broad numbers of people that they can no longer live in the old way, that the risk of change is less than the risk of continuing as we are.
- Revolutionary organizations capable of focusing the aspirations and energy of the people, ensuring that their struggle doesn't get diverted, dissipated or co-opted.

The existence of these conditions doesn't guarantee a revolution. Throughout history, there have been times when they have been present, but revolutions did not occur. But no radical transformation of any society has ever occurred without them.

We don't have much control over the first two. They're developing without our help, inexorably and naturally as the global economic system slides ever deeper into structural crisis.

The existence of the third condition is entirely in our hands, and our responsibility to bring about. If we don't develop a solid revolutionary movement with a viable strategy, the consequences will be ugly indeed.

Capitalists will never relax in their quest for ever more profit and power. If we are to ever emancipate ourselves, we must find within ourselves that same relentless determination that our enemy possesses. We should constantly seek and seize every opportunity to advance, to the maximum extent possible within whatever conditions we face.

Revolution is the violent overthrow of one class by another.

There's no way around this hard truth.

People associated with a multitude of political trends claim to desire radical change, but turn back when faced with the necessity of revolution. They want desperately to believe that we can achieve a just, sustainable society without resorting to violence.

But it is inescapable that "political power grows out of the barrel of a gun." Violence is merely one of many tools that we need to use, but if we put that one back in the box, we will fail. More to the point: there is no moral high ground in refusing to fight to emancipate ourselves, in refusing to defend ourselves against the colossal violence that this system perpetrates ceaselessly.

Aside from sociopaths and capitalists, humans generally have a strong aversion to conflict and bloodshed. One of the reasons we hate capitalism is precisely because it is so horrifically violent. It will commit any atrocity for profit—wars, starvation, mass extinctions, toxifying the food chain. Those who run the system don't care about life, and will stop at nothing. No living being is left in peace if it can be monetized in some way. This system imposes its imperative on everyone: participate or die.

We need to face the scope of this problem. Before we can even discuss tactics, we need to understand our true situation. This expansionist global economic system is killing the planet. It is the mortal enemy of anyone who values life and desires an end to exploitation. It needs to be stopped, yesterday.

Tactics are a secondary concern, and should be employed strate-

gically. Asking people to consider various strategies and tactics is secondary to coming to agreement about our objectives.

An international revolutionary movement led by the working class would necessarily incorporate a range of tactics. Successful movements for change have historically comprised wide ranges of people focusing on different aspects. All types of tactics are employed to contribute to a common goal.

But we can not leave out the question of political power. This is decisive. Exclusively non-violent tactics will not persuade the bourgeoisie to stop converting life into profit. They will continue to exercise the power to exploit, backed up by armies, police, political and cultural institutions, until they are forced to stop.

We have learned many times through history that whenever non-violent resistance movements begin to be effective, they are promptly attacked, and compelled to either defend themselves or submit to repression. When resistance movements succeed, it is because they are backed up by force or the threat of force. England wouldn't have given the pacifist Gandhi the time of day if they weren't trying to suppress a rising revolutionary movement in India. They chose him in order to marginalize (and defeat) the revolution for full independence, recognizing him as someone they could make a deal with so they could continue to exploit India in a neo-colonialist framework.

A forceful nonviolent movement could help destabilize the corporate centers of power. But it can not be the decisive factor in defeating these centers. They will not hesitate to annihilate anyone who truly threatens their rule. We must be able to fight to win. We can't do this with one hand ideologically tied behind our backs, with a range of tactics unavailable to us due to pacifist dogmatism.

REVOLUTION IN 3 SIMPLE STEPS: AFFIRM, CONSOLIDATE, STRUGGLE

Building a movement requires three basic, interconnected activities:

1. Affirmation: raise consciousness.
2. Consolidation: organize forces.
3. Struggle.

Though one flows into another, these steps are not strictly sequential. They are employed simultaneously, blending into and building upon one another in a mutually-reinforcing (dialectical) process. For example, in order to take action against the enemy, one must already have some adequate number of class-conscious and organized forces. In turn, potential new recruits are drawn in through the thick of struggle, and the cycle begins anew. With each turn, an organization builds its strength, allowing it to escalate its engagement with the enemy until the ultimate showdown.

First, revolutionary consciousness is foundational. Before revolution can happen in real life, its possibility must be acknowledged in the mind. Of primary importance right now is building unity around the fact that various social and political struggles are connected, and that solving any of them requires addressing the entire system.

Theory and ideological unity develop from (and along with) the motion of reality itself. Instead of dogmas, formulas, fantasies and other concoctions of the imagination, we need to examine what actually exists in front of us, and construct theory that is based on our situation.

We need to shake off the lies and illusions so we can understand exactly what we're dealing with. In order to challenge the current order, millions of people must know in their bones that this system is our mortal enemy and can not be reformed.

Second, we need to construct various forms of self-replicating, autonomous yet interconnected organizations. These ought to be structured with the capacity to deal with our current conditions, and as much as possible like the society we are aiming for.

Individually we can't change society — this must be done collectively. Within our strategic alliances, we must be mutually supportive and set aside secondary conflicts and contradictions. We have to maintain principled (non-opportunist) unity, even with people we don't particularly like.

We have to build up our collective capacity to act through struggle, starting small and initially only taking on what we can win. We need to develop stamina for the long road we have to travel, before we reach a point where we can damage, weaken, and ultimately halt the production of capital.

Until a revolutionary situation ripens (and it will), we need to focus all our energies on preparing for it. Then when uprisings fill the streets and events spiral out of control, people will know what side they are on and what must be done, and most crucially, we will have the ability to do it.

The consequences of not being prepared are dire. The people may rise up spontaneously, but if we are not prepared ideologically and organizationally, we will be defeated or co-opted, and nothing will substantially change.

AFFIRMATION: AGITATION & PROPAGANDA

Brief definitions:

Affirmation: Spreading a message through agitation and propaganda.

Agitation: A general message directed to a relatively broad section of people. It usually exposes the crimes of the enemy, and is intended to agitate, to stir emotion.

Propaganda: A more specific message directed to a relatively narrower section of people. It uses theory to increase the level of understanding about a phenomenon.

Affirmation and consolidation are contradictory yet mutually necessary imperatives; one is spreading outward to find people so we can grow, and the other is solidifying our unity to strengthen ourselves organizationally. Each has to advance in its turn, or both will stagnate.

The purpose of agitation is to organize. If we affirm without consolidating, we'll be stuck as a few exhausted people who distribute leaflets or build up a website, with no organization. If we focus on consolidating our organization but neglect affirmation, we'll end up with a few highly unified individuals, but won't be able to grow. Either way, we end up with a "head without a body."

Theory: foundational hypothesis about how the world or society works. Examples:
- "Our destiny is determined by the Flying Spaghetti Monster."
- "The Earth is being destroyed because of corporate greed."
- "Capitalism impels perpetual industrial growth. Ecocide is an effect of capitalism."

Ideology: a set of convictions comprising an approach to life. Examples:

- "We should not question the Flying Spaghetti Monster."
- "Corporations have too much power."
- "Our enemy is the capitalist class."

Political Line: our general trajectory or "line of march," which determines an approach to action on specific topics. Examples:

- "We should pray to the Flying Spaghetti Monster every night."
- "To reform capitalism, we should limit the power of corporations."
- "To destroy capitalism, the working class must organize to seize the means of production."

Starting from scratch

Even if you're alone, you can start to organize.

The first step is affirmation. Methods include:

- Leafletting at events or in neighborhoods
- Online discussion
- Host open activities, such as lectures or film showings
- Attend events and talk to people

If anyone agrees with you, or expresses something similar, then you can ask them if you can have a one-on-one conversation, to determine what your unity is and how you might be able to work together.

The next step is to meet with them and see if they agree to build an organization with you. The level would be based on what you agree on. It might take a bunch of long meetings to define and determine what that is; this is to be expected.

You can come up with a set of points that you want to hammer out together. Instead of coming to it with pre-determined expectations or worked-out programmes, if we work together on making decisions, then we will build stronger organizations. We can't do anything, even if we have great ideas, without finding people and working with them directly as they are (with all our strengths, weaknesses, and level of understanding). Part of what we're doing is transforming ourselves as *people*, not just changing systems, so that we all can become fit to run society when we get the chance. So we start with people as we/they are and build from there.

If we try something and it doesn't work, that's fine. Being wrong is not a problem, if we learn from it. We need to experiment and try many different things. We're in a totally new and different situation. We can't learn how to play the guitar very well without a lot of practice, and the same is true of organizing.

If you get even one or two more people to agree to work with you, then you all can start by calling for broader meetings to discuss topics that will help develop a movement. To keep the parameters of the discussion focused on what you want to talk about, and not have to argue about the premises you're starting with (which would fatally drive down the level of conversation), at first invite specific people who are on a similar wavelength. Rather than sit in front of the room telling people what you think they should do, this is an opportunity to exchange ideas, strategize and brainstorm together.

Unity-Struggle-Unity

Unity-struggle-unity is a method of working together.

Principled unity is not the same thing as compromise. It also doesn't demand that everyone think the same way (which is, in any case, impossible). Principled unity defines areas of common ground, upon which common work can be based, without requiring anyone to suppress or hide their disagreements. It allows for non-antagonistic discussion of differences (which are not considered negative, but illuminating), with the purpose of coming to increasing agreement and raising the level of unity. Then new differences will emerge at a yet higher level. This back-and-forth process is called "unity-struggle-unity" and is a method of working together with mutual respect and influence, each testing one's own ideas against the ideas of others, with the possibility of increasing common ground.

The Mass Line

The mass line refers to the method of constructing a political line through the dialectical (back-and-forth) relationship between an organization and the masses, particularly the working class. The theory guiding working class struggle, and the practice of organizations, originates in the working class. (Because of ideological domination, it may not happen spontaneously). An organization gathers specific empirical observations and experiences, and synthesizes or rationalizes them into general principles. These in turn are used to guide future practice among and with the masses. It is through this constant process of exchange, of the concentration from specific to general, and back again from general to specific, that proletarian theory can become a social force.

Theory + Practice = Praxis

The purpose of theory is practice. We don't need to interpret and understand reality for its own sake, but to act upon and affect it. Our presence and actions always affect reality (positively or negatively) no matter what. Left to spontaneity, this usually occurs in ways that reflect our conditioning by our class enemy, and serves them. Proletarian theory allows us to affect reality in a more conscious way, in accordance with our own class interests.

Like jam on toast, theory and practice are inseparable. (Try it. Try scraping ALL the jam off a piece of toast.) Their integration is essential. Toast without jam is dry and flavorless; so is theory. Jam by itself is a gooey blob; likewise practice without theory is aimless activism.

It's common wisdom that we learn by doing. You can read about painting, write about it, obsess about it during every waking hour, but you're not a painter until you mess around with actual paint. You can not understand the properties of your materials, how they work, through contemplation. Paintings never turn out exactly the way they're envisioned. Only by picking up the brush and applying it can you learn what works and what doesn't, and move beyond speculation and fantasy into something real.

Doing without thinking isn't much better. Not only does your painting turn out like crap, but you're encouraging others to churn out crap as well.

Theory isn't static formula — it's interpretation of experience, observation and practice, continuously adapting and modifying to fit the structured unpredictability of real life. In turn, theory gives direction to our practice. We experiment to see what works and what doesn't, and we incorporate that back into our theory.

In the dynamic, non-linear, back-and-forth dialectic of theory and practice, practice is primary. Nothing changes without action. If we act, even lashing out on instinct without an articulated or conscious theory, at least something happens (for good or ill). And though our instincts are badly atrophied and manipulated by the prevailing system, they're often right.

Practice shouldn't be defined narrowly — it's not just a matter of protesting or marching or whatever you do outside in public. Every type of activity is a form of practice, even articulating theory itself. More important than its form is whether or not it's strategic, directed toward and getting us closer to our goal.

Class position determines ideas

Theory does not belong to any individual, but is constructed through class struggle, and is comprised of our collective interpretation of experiences and observations. This is true even if it is articulated by particular individuals. Historically, when individuals have contributed significantly to proletarian theory and have been able to exert social influence as a result, they have done so not as isolated "great" individuals above everyone else — instead they synthesized what they observed in the social realm as a whole, what many others were doing and thinking.

There has been a widespread misconception that because theory has been articulated by individuals, that it comes from outside the class struggle (specifically from petit bourgeois intellectuals to the proletariat). This is an erroneous, idealist view. Proletarian theory is always constructed through the actual struggles of the proletariat, even when intellectuals with origins outside the proletariat have synthesized these experiences and articulated the resulting theoretical concepts.

CONSOLIDATION: ORGANIZATION IS POWER

The point is power

Organization has one purpose: to exercise collective power. For individuals, it is necessary to unite with others to assert and magnify power beyond personal limits. The more highly organized a section of people is, the more social power they are able to exert.

What is the exercise of power? It is the willful imposition of control; in our case, action intended to transform the status quo, to subvert and replace it.

The inertia of a society, the motion, mechanisms and traditions that are in place, establish the direction of that society. Under global capitalism, the direction is one way: continuous and intensified exploitation and omnicide.

The system is highly organized

Class society is highly organized, increasingly so as it has developed through global capitalism and beyond. It has constructed political institutions to exert its power in every realm of activity. The state is just one form, with its major power tools the military and police, along with its courts, legislatures, down to the smallest government office in the smallest town. There is also economic power, controlling the ways we can fulfill our basic needs (starting with land, and later the development and control of all means of production). Once they control what we need to survive, then the dominant classes can threaten to withhold these necessities unless we agree to participate in our own exploitation through wage labor. Power is asserted ideologically: through the culture, the media, the arts, which each persuade us, with varying degrees of subtlety, that this is the best of all possible social arrangements. This lie is also asserted through oppressive structures such as the family, patriarchy, and racism.

The system defines the limits of our activity at a social level. As part of overcoming capital, we struggle against the power of the system to impose these limits. They pacify and disorganize us at every turn; we exist as a social force only insofar as we ourselves are organized, autonomous, and active.

Coercion is invisible from the inside

The power of the system is a net that has woven itself into the very personality of the majority of the people living within it. So much so that many people can not even perceive its existence. Instead, it seems natural like air, or like water to fish. Because of its seeming "naturalness" and its inertia, and the inexorable weight of its motion, cooperation with it becomes spontaneous. The thoughts and actions of those subjected to the system's conditioning, those who are integrated within it and have come to identify with it, are likely to remain stable unless something, or someone, intervenes.

Oppression breeds resistance

Because class society is not in fact natural, is in fact anti-nature and against human nature (we evolved in cooperative and collective bands), it automatically generates resistance. The form that this takes is determined by class consciousness. In the conditioned subject, this impulse to resist gets diverted and misdirected back into the system's own mechanisms (such as elections), provide space to blow off steam (ie: sports, demonstrations), and are also deflected back into the subject, creating self-hatred, depression and horizontal hostility (antagonism between sections of the dominated classes).

The power the rulers exert must be relentless. If they relax the pressure for one second, or allow solutions to become clear (for instance, if resistance, instead of being diverted, actually achieved any kind of victory that could be emulated), or allow any outside intervention to occur, then its subjects can be shaken out of their conditioning. This possibility, from the system's point of view, must not be permitted to be realized.

But as the declining system begins to fragment more rapidly, its illegitimacy at every level becomes increasingly evident. People begin to wake up in spite of the social control mechanisms. Then the system increasingly turns to backup methods to enforce its power: overt repression and terror.

Alone, we're helpless

Without organizations, the power of an individual to fight back is extremely limited or non-existent. We are permitted to possess power only in relation to others even lower on the social hierarchy. Men are generally allowed to abuse women. Parents can control their children. But no one is allowed to harm the profits of a corporation.

We can't expect to defeat such a highly organized and powerful enemy if we are not organized and collectively able to exert power.

Those in power understand that very well.

Look how much effort they focus on breaking up any forms of organization that don't reinforce their rule. Churches, sports leagues and the Boy Scouts may organize unmolested by the state, because these all direct us to serve the bourgeoisie. But the state diverts (or crushes if necessary) not only organizations that resist, but those that even question their right to rule and exploit.

Stepping out of line is met with overt or covert repression:

- The genocide of indigenous people who refuse(d) to surrender and assimilate.
- The assault on workers organizations from Day One of capitalism.
- The obsessive and increasingly sophisticated and widespread surveillance, infiltration and disruption of dissenting groups.
- The overblown fear campaigns against capitalism's enemies — Red Scare, Green Scare, War on Terror.

Not only do those in power attack organizations, but in addition, they use numerous means to keep us from getting together in the first place:

- Workers have been dispersed away from industrial centers.
- Students have been dispersed off campuses and toward on-line education.
- Suburbia was built to pull people out of city centers.
- Isolating technologies like iPods are pushed as indispensable.
- Public spaces like town squares and parks have been removed.
- Public transportation has been allowed to degrade or has been largely eliminated (this was not exclusively about selling more cars).

Without organization, we have nothing

It is only by the coordinated force of an organized people that this system can be effectively challenged. We need to grasp this fact as well as our adversaries do. The more organized we are, the more powerful we become.

The power of the system means that they can exploit and rob us at will. If we don't have power, all we can do is complain, resist futilely, or comply.

The power of the system means that they can kill us and make us sick by poisoning our air, water and soil. If we had power, we could put a stop to it. Without power, all we can do is individually try to avoid the ever-more-pervasive threats to our well-being.

What is organization?

It means connecting — building relationships — in order to act collectively for a common purpose.

Because our purpose goes against spontaneity (the system's cultural and ideological hegemony), it must involve discussion, sharing and struggle of ideas (theory/ideology/politics). We must constantly question, examine and challenge the dominant ideas within our own thinking so that we can develop methods and approaches that are truly oppositional, that do not inadvertently echo the interests of the ruling class. To constantly battle their ideological hegemony, we must challenge each other, and to do this we practice criticism/self-criticism.

We need organization to increase the power of the dominated classes so we can overturn the system of domination. This necessitates common work. It is only through practice that we can formulate correct ideas. It is only through practice that we can learn how to wield power. And it's only through assembling sufficient forces, and applying ourselves in a combative way, that we can exert our collective power effectively enough to win.

Organization against the system necessarily begins small. But it bubbles up in many locations at once, because the workings of the system itself cause people to talk, work together, try to figure out what to do. We build and learn to exert our own power through fighting the dominant power. This is all one process.

As they grow, the organizations that correspond more closely to the demands of the times, to reality, tend to attract more people. Organizations may merge, or connect in other ways. Alliances will form even among diverse groups, of various sizes and formations, with distinct goals and ideas. They will form movements. Within movements will be organizations at various levels and of various capabilities and with different foci.

Eventually they will, together, become strong enough to challenge the system.

They don't have to be a majority to get to this point, though there must be active support by a significant section of the population. So a minority must continuously (even if not linearly) develop strength and numbers, through increasing levels of struggle, while honing a strategy and tactics that can win.

They start from a position of defense. As they go on the offense and demonstrate strength, a correct political line, and the ability to win — and just as importantly, as the system demonstrates increasing evilness and weakness — then they attract ever more people.

Capitalism will defend itself to the death, and we will have to fight hard and smart. So we will need armed forces, political forces, and ideological forces that can assert our position and ultimately defeat the enemy on all fronts.

We—all the dominated masses—must unite if we are to defeat our common enemy: the capitalist/imperialist system. We need to build combative organizations internationally, to fight for our interests against an enemy that is also organized on a global scale. Together we can emancipate ourselves and transform society, to end domination and exploitation.

Physical meetings are required.

Exchanging ideas and information online is an essential part of building organization. But this is extremely limited, especially since we know that everything online (plus mail and phones) is monitored. We also need to meet with one another, face to face. We need to know the individuals we're working with and relying on in the real world, especially as we navigate the building of movements together. We need to be familiar with their ideas, political background and viewpoints not only as they are self-asserted in words, but also as they play out in practice.

It takes time and mutual experience to develop trust. Someone can appear to be the most militant revolutionary online, and turn out to be a complete flake when more is required than typing at a desk. We need to struggle together, to get proficient at what we're trying to do, to make our minor mistakes before the stakes rise too high to allow for experimentation. We need to gather now to develop and act on our collective line, strategy, and plans, so that we will be ready as possibilities arise for advancing the struggle.

Organization can only be forged through real-life struggle, through common practice and theoretical work.

Our choice as militants: revolutionary or progressive?

As all of us who are part of the popular masses unite against our common enemy, each of us must choose at what level we will do so. This is ultimately determined by our ideological position (which is strongly affected, but not inevitably fixed, by our economic position). Essentially, our choice is to operate either as a progressive or as a revolutionary.

Progressives:
contribute to the advancement of history in general compatibility with the interests of the proletariat, in a relationship of some level of guidance or leadership from the working class in struggle.

Revolutionaries:
directly participate in investing time and energy for the proletarian alternative to triumph.

Most of those who are not workers, not part of the process of producing surplus value, but are still part of the "popular masses" will operate in the progressive camp. The long-term unemployed, or non-productive (service) employees, or students, or other members of the progressive or radical petit bourgeoisie can't touch capital; can't get their hands on it. They can't go on strike to make it stop reproducing itself. This doesn't make it impossible to be a proletarian revolutionary, but it does present challenges.

If we in those categories (as a cartoonist/writer that definitely includes me) are to be part of the proletarian revolutonary alternative, we must disrobe/strip ourselves of our petit bourgeois origin. We must, in other words, abandon our class interests and dedicate ourselves fully to the interests of the working class. This is a long and difficult process. It is usually ultimately unsuccessful; most will travel the revolutionary path part of the way, and then jump off when it gets too hard.

But even then, those who are in the various sections of the petit bourgeoisie can still contribute by organizing at the progressive level, build alliances to expose and resist various forms of domination by capital, as well as its effects, and organize support and solidarity for autonomous working class struggles. Mobilizing as a means of building mass movements is positive and necessary. Strategically blocking the flow of capital and resource extraction can complement and enhance struggles at the point of production. There is a lot that anyone can do to damage capital, and capitalism, and we should strive to maximize all of our efforts in that direction.

Levels of organization[9]

There are three basic levels of organization (each divisible into more specific layers): revolutionary, intermediate and mass.

These categories, defined by levels of consciousness and commitment, are not rigid, and a group can blend them or change from one to another according to circumstances. Their relationship is dialectical, each level acting upon and influencing the others. Their boundaries are permeable, with individuals able to move from one level to another, or to operate in more than one at a time. Some of their elements differ only in degree or emphasis.Each level must function autonomously and to its own fullest potential.

The levels are generally characterized as follows:

Revolutionary organization:

The revolutionary level is principal. This type of organization is indispensible and ultimately determinate — without its presence, the other two tend to lose themselves in the murky dead ends of spontaneity, reformism and economism (reducing and limiting the struggle to trade unionism). It has:

- A high level of theoretical, ideological and political unity.
- A common long-term goal, a comprehensive strategy, and a detailed plan to implement that strategy.
- Continuously developing methods of work, and systematic summation of that work.
- A process, honed through practice, of collectively shaping ideas, direction and policies.
- A membership of cadre who have dedicated their lives to the struggle.
- A structure that is configured to withstand repression.

Mass organization:

Mass organizations are currently instruments of struggle to weaken the capitalist class. After the defeat of capital, they will be instruments of power for a revolutionary state. Their characteristics:

- Unity based on common interests to achieve specific goals (such as a union fighting for higher wages, students for free education, or a coalition to stop a war).
- Ideologically and politically broad, often vague or populist.
- A simple goal and/or strategy, usually limited to one issue, often short-term.
- Membership requirements are loose, and expectations are not

strict.
- A basically open structure — anyone can join.

Intermediate organization:

The intermediate level organization is a tool with which we can build a combative mass movement that unites all who can be united to fight the system. It can create more favorable conditions for mass struggle, and be in place when mass struggle does erupt, to maximize its effectiveness and provide continuity through its inevitable ebbs and flows.

It can also locate and train radicals who might also begin to organize at the revolutionary level.

The intermediate level organization is neither a revolutionary organization nor a mass organization, nor a midde-of-the-road blend. It has unique characteristics distinct from both. It operates between the two, structurally and ideologically, and links them.

As its own autonomous level, it has three general areas of activity:

1) to resist capitalist domination and its effects
2) to weaken capital
3) to support mass struggles of the working class against exploitation and imperialism

It has:

- A progressive level of unity that defines and opposes the system as a whole, yet refrains from defining a specific strategy for eliminating it (thus is able to embrace members with various theories).

- A goal of uniting all who can be united for a medium-range goal (the precise content of which is not fixed, but dependent upon historical circumstances and the changing level of class consciousness among the masses—for example, it could currently be to defeat global capitalism) without attempting to unify on long-term goals (such as the precise form of a future society).
- Collectivity in developing common plans and tactics for achieving the medium-range goal.
- A non-sectarian and mutually supportive orientation.
- A process of continuously improving methods and practice through collective summation.
- A membership with some level of accountability and commitment beyond "weekend warrior."
- A semi-open or invitation-only (but not clandestine) structure.

Organizing explicitly at the intermediate level can prevent the problems that occur when a group calling itself either a revolutionary or a mass organization is, in reality, mushing the levels together. Though the intermediate level organization is not widely understood, it is widely practiced (usually unknowingly). If a group proclaims to be revolutionary but hasn't yet achieved the degree of unity and commitment that revolutionary practice requires, then it is in fact an intermediary organization. If a group is attempting to build a mass organization but doesn't yet have a mass base, then it is in fact an intermediate level organization.

[9] This section is excerpted from (and revised): *Toward an Anti-Capitalist/Anti-Imperialist Mass Movement: Organizing at the Intermediate Level,* One Struggle, September 2011, http://onestruggle.net/2011/09/02/toward-an-anti-capitalistanti-imperialist-mass-movement-organizing-at-the-intermediate-level/

Being a revolutionary militant requires tremendous sacrifice, resolve, persistence, and hard work. It ends in violent death or prison.
Your recruitment pitch could use some work.

STRUGGLE

We're already at war

We're always in engagement with the enemy. Usually that consists of them dominating, oppressing and exploiting us. Did you just eat some of their commodified food? Buy one of their products? Work one of their jobs? Hum one of their advertising jingles? That's domination.

Class struggle is always occurring, in every corner of our society and lives—even in our own thinking. We constantly struggle to be human beings in the face of their efforts to turn us into machines or useless dross.

What we need to do, through organization, is collectivize that struggle so that we might have a chance of winning.

There are no formulas or programmes that can help us predict the forms of struggle that we need to engage in. We must face our specific conditions, whatever they are and as they constantly change.

Organization and struggle have an interconnected (dialectical) relationship, with our level of organization determining how we wage struggles, and our struggles in turn contributing toward building organization.

We should wage struggles that are correspondent to our organizational capacity.

Several principles can be applied:

1) Don't act above our capacity. If we attempt to advance beyond our capacity, without the ability to defend our gains or retreat

when necessary, then we will be easily crushed.

2) Don't act below our capacity. We should constantly seek and seize every opportunity to advance our struggles and weaken the enemy, to the maximum extent possible in whatever conditions we face (while preserving our organizations).

3) If we are to ever emancipate ourselves, we must possess even more relentless determination and strength than our enemy does. We need to outwit them. Be brave, strong, relentless, and smart.

4) Practice makes perfect, and builds confidence. We should take every opportunity (even small, insignificant ones) to speak our mind, to stand up for our rights, to assert our class interests. Conflict becomes less frightening and we become more skilled at it.

5) Similarly, practice collectivity. Even if something might be easier to accomplish alone, find someone else to work with. The point is not just completing tasks (though that is important), but how we strengthen ourselves collectively through the process.

6) Always put the needs and interests of the collective first.

7) Build up our particular skills to serve the struggle. Developing our individual capacity in public speaking, constructing theory, debate, speaking more languages, fundraising, publicity, hosting events, and so on, is useful for the collective.

8) Anticipate future conditions. Don't be careless today just because it might not have immediate consequences, when similar behavior might lead to your defeat tomorrow.

TRAPS, PITFALLS AND DEAD ENDS

In spite of all our good intentions, more often than not we wind up acting as the unwitting footsoldiers of capital. They are masterful at manipulating all forms of resistance in ways that feed back into and reinforce the system.

Capitalism fosters ideologies among its opposition that brings us right back into their embrace. Because the people's camp is generally disorganized and there's a low level of political consciousness, we are susceptible to capitalist recuperation if we're not constantly on guard against it.

The only way we can prevent this is to always keep uppermost in mind the fundamental contradiction of capitalism: capital vs. labor. If we use that dividing line between the fundamental classes as our guide, our North star, then we can stay solidly on our path.

There are several major deviations from a proletarian line that widely afflict the people's camp, even as we resist the various attacks of capitalism. These, even when they appear "radical," represent petit bourgeois ideology, because they target the effects of capital rather than its core, its cause, and therefore they can not lead to the defeat of capitalism.

Awareness of these pitfalls is crucial because capitalism has so many methods of assimilating our struggles, and we have to make sure we don't get sidetracked. The system is usually five steps ahead of us, having figured out how to divert our righteous discontent into forms that reinforce its own institutions. These are very sophisticated and persuasive—they make us feel that we're making a difference when in fact we're tightening the bonds of our own oppression.

All these forms are basically varieties of reformism, because that's all they ultimately lead to. They are where resistance goes to die.

Reformism: is the ideology that capitalism can be made "less evil," or less destructive, through reforms, without smashing it. To be clear: fighting for reforms, if one element of an overall revolutionary strategy, is not the same as reform*ism*. Reformism elevates these struggles to an ideology that poses reform as the goal itself. We should encourage and assist combative mass organizations to fight for reforms that weaken capital, without sinking into reformism and getting stuck there.

Mass organizations under this system (such as collaborationist unions and NGOs) are usually dominated by institutionalized bureaucracies whose very functions are, first: to make money, and second: to pacify the masses by diverting their discontent into compromises with capital.

Many of them are funded by capitalist entities, turning political organizing into jobs involving social work or charity, and the organized into passive recipients of assistance.

The non-funded ones tend to lack continuity: they are able to mobilize people for brief spurts but then lose support as issues fade.

Mass organizations, by providing no analysis of the systemic nature of the world's problems, are unable to break the system's ideological hegemony. Instead, if the revolutionary level is not present to prevent this, politicians and other professional reformists glom onto these organizations and suck the life out of them, channeling sincere people into pointless, energy-draining, losing strategies that objectively defend the interests of various sectors of capitalism and ensure its reproduction.

Elections, corporate-funded nonprofits, NGOs and CBOs, personal lifestyle changes, political pressure, petitions, culture-jamming, tinkering with the economy, green jobs, withdrawing our

support, symbolic protests — all are offered up as options for dissent. None of them are sufficient; on the contrary, they serve to reinforce the system's authority and the illusion of democracy.

These misguided approaches have traction because most people don't grasp how the system actually works, and that it is structurally unreformable. They don't recognize capitalism as the absolute enemy that it is.

The major flaw of environmentalists and, frankly, the labor movement as well (which has mostly been co-opted by collaborationist unions) has been a lack of class analysis and understanding of capitalism as a system that we need to defeat. Instead, many participants in these struggles fall victim to illusions.

Organizations that do have a political line correctly identifying the contradiction between capital and labor are still subject to petit bourgeois ideology, which centers on individualism.

Individualism: prioritizing one's perceived immediate personal interests above collective interests.

Reformism and individualism have many forms, all rooted in the failure to identify capitalism's fundamental contradiction.

Forms of reformism and individualism:

Activism: action for action's sake. An activist is an ambulance chaser, dissipating energy by running from campaign to campaign without integrating their work into a long-term strategy.

Dogmatism: rigid adherence to stagnant theory. A dogmatist will use quotations to make an argument (if so-and-so said it, then it's true). Dogma is dead theory; it doesn't develop with reality.

Sectarianism: refusal to find principled ways of uniting with others in the movement. Sectarians will compete for converts rather than combine efforts.

Horizontal hostility: attacking others in the movement, in a failure to distinguish between "contradictions among the people," and "contradictions between the people and the enemy."

Lifestyleism: focusing on changing one's personal behaviors, in the belief that if everyone did so, society would be improved. Capitalism can't be boycotted from existence, or starved by any consumer choice we can possibly make.

Populism: appealing to the concerns of "the people" as a whole, while erasing or ignoring classes. This can mislead the masses into fighting against their own interests.

Pragmatism: acting in ways that don't correspond with a political line or objective. Going with the flow.

Opportunism: compromising with the enemy by watering down one's own views.

Blaming the people: claiming that the problem is consumerism, or the ignorance of the masses. The masses did not put the system in place, don't control it, and are its victims.

189

Unity without autonomy: being a footsoldier for someone else's agenda.

Working with liberals and reformists can be an exercise in frustration, but we can't prevail without winning many over to our side. We should only engage in common work with them when we are organized enough to insist that our politics are represented.

Our progressive and revolutionary organizations must be autonomous, and have a strategy and plan for how to ensure that our point of view remains part of the mix of any open group, assembly or coalition. There is a spontaneous, irresistible tendency for a broad open group to adopt reformist, lowest-common-denominator politics, and if we don't insist on an autonomous presence, we will be swallowed and digested. This happens because

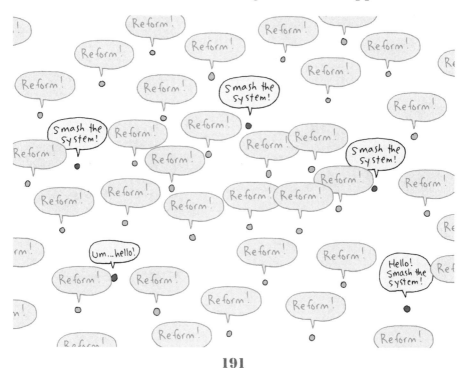

reformism is the political position that corresponds to the petit bourgeoisie, which is the class of most activists and organizers today (even those who appear very "radical"). Unlike the proletariat, the petit bourgeoisie doesn't have a direct material interest in revolution, and so their solutions will be centered around reforming the system. This isn't surprising or bad; it simply is something we have to deal with and take into account.

Many of them would like to see a better world, but most will ultimately resist revolution even more than the crimes of capitalism. They'll often do this by exhibiting moral outrage against violence, especially when advocated or employed as a tool for resistance or revolution. (Everyday counter-revolutionary violence usually gets a pass). They are just privileged enough to prefer the continuation of this murderous, ecocidal system, over a war of liberation in which they risk losing what they have.

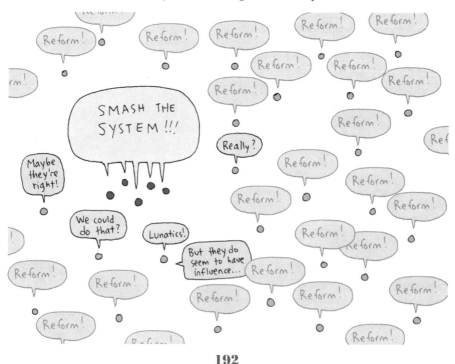

NGO activists, liberals, politicians, and other militant moderates tend to overrun open coalitions, and then band together to silence or ignore any suggestions outside the bounds of reformism. They will bleed out the progressive or revolutionary content of any endeavor, and turn it into an advocacy group that somehow serves capitalist interests, even if in a roundabout way.

This will usually be the general course of any new mass mobilization or organization, unless the revolutionary and/or intermediate (progressive) levels are present, alert and assertive about offering an alternative.

Most people don't see anything wrong with this, and so it is difficult to prevent. After all, why would the average liberal activist question the common sense impulse to invite every known group to participate, with as many members as they can bring? Who but a nitpicking curmudgeon would argue against being "inclusive"? Who wants to hear (or be the one to say) that their actions are not going to really solve the problem? At least they're doing *something*, which is better than nothing... right?

Even taking all this into account, it is important to remember that reformists are not our enemy (at this time). We must approach them with patience and without antagonism, striving to win as many as possible over to the side of the working class. We'll have to win them over again and again and again, all the way through the revolutionary process, until at the end, the majority of them are destined to betray us and seek refuge under the wing of the bourgeoisie. Since this has occurred many times historically, we can anticipate it with a fair amount of certainty. But we must keep in mind that during particular stages of the struggle, our success could hinge on their support, even if half-hearted.

Targeting effects rather than cause

War. Ecocide. Poverty. Exploitation. Police brutality. Rape. Prisons. Torture. Racism. The list of crimes committed in the service of capitalism is horrifying, endless, and overwhelming.

It's very compelling to address each one on its own terms. For example, if we believe that our most urgent concern is to stop the destruction of the planet (without which any gains in social justice will be meaningless), we might direct our energy toward organizing environmentalists against raw materials extraction (by blocking fracking, coal trains or oil pipelines, for example).

But even if some of those campaigns are successful, that won't be enough, or even close. Capitalism can easily absorb any particular (and it's always temporary) loss and flow around it. Case in point: while many people have been busy resisting the Keystone XL tar sands oil pipeline, energy companies have built other pipeline and rail transport networks with even greater capacity.

Ecocide (quickly leading to omnicide) is an effect of capitalism, of commodity production. It is an extremely dire consequence, but nevertheless peripheral to the generation of capital. In order to stop ecocide, the generation of capital itself must be halted, at its core, its source: the production of surplus value through the exploitation of labor.

There is no quick fix. To end any of capitalism's atrocities, we must push forward and rupture its fundamental inner contradiction. The only ones who can ultimately defeat capital are those who, through being enslaved to it, produce it: the working class. We need to build a movement capable of overturning the entire system, all the forms of domination that keep it in place, the entire matrix of social relations that comprise it.

195

Identity politics

Capitalists use various forms of oppression of particular social categories to solidify their rule over society as a whole, for the ultimate purpose of reinforcing class domination. Reserving special forms of hell for certain sections of people makes the masses easier to control. In addition, dividing the working class against itself ideologically (fostering racism, xenophobia, misogyny, homophobia) also makes it easier to control the class as a whole, and to squeeze more surplus value out of it (which is the only thing they really care about, their sole purpose and aim).

Social categories are not the same as classes. Groups defined by gender, nationality, skin pigmentation and so on cut across class lines — they can be members of any class, even when they are mainly pushed into one or another class. They are either oppressed or relatively privileged based on these identity categories, a condition distinct from their class position defined by their relationship to production.

While fighting against and ending oppression is crucial, focusing the struggle on it does not address the fundamental contradiction of capitalism, and thus cannot end either classes or oppression. Oppression can change (be ameliorated or shift to other groups) without threatening the existence of capitalism. Capitalism is capable of absorbing the enlargement of democratic rights under the continued dictatorship of the bourgeoisie. For oppression to end, it must be addressed within the overall context of class struggle.

Brief definitions:

Domination: an ensemble of relations involving economic, political and ideological power of one group over another.

Power: the capacity to achieve one's aims, which may or may not entail prevailing against another's interests or will.

Exploitation: paying less for labor power than the exchange value of the product of that labor.

Oppression: the systematic subordination of specific social categories, which can involve structurally unequal conditions and rights.

Repression: the use of force (or threats of force) for the purpose of domination.

"For the propertied bourgeois woman, her house is the world...

... For the proletarian woman, the whole world is her house."

Rosa Luxemburg

Feminism doesn't go far enough.

Feminism (more precisely, bourgeois feminism) is the struggle for gender equality — particularly equal rights. It does not address the framework in which inequality exists, does not challenge the system as a whole. Radical feminism (which is still reformist in spite of its name) asserts, further, that the oppression of women by men (aka patriarchy) is the fundamental or central form of domination that exists in human society. There are clear differences between these ideologies and proletarian ideology, which asserts that the fundamental form of domination in capitalist society is that of the capitalist class over the working class, and thus insists upon struggling against all forms of oppression in the context of class struggle — in the process of overturning capitalism, rather than confining our goal to achieving equality within it.

Of course, class society from its inception has been intertwined with the oppression of women. The division of labor based on gender within some hunter-forager societies may have laid the groundwork for class divisions to develop in the first place. But as classes emerged, these became the fundamental divisions in society, which shape and determine the others, and have to be overcome for the others to be resolved. Classes are social forces in struggle based on their relation to production. Genders are not classes, but cross-class social categories.

All the forms of oppression and domination and destruction that are perpetrated by capitalist society must be confronted and dealt with in the process of defeating capitalism. Contrary to what some class reductionists assert, we must not wait to deal with them until "after" class emancipation, or we will never achieve it. (There's no such thing as partial revolution — it's all or nothing). But at the same time, they can't be resolved outside the process of class struggle. Class emancipation includes and encompasses smashing oppression as well as exploitation.

Like all forms of oppression, the oppression of women serves the class in power, and harms everyone else (not only women). Though it targets women in particular, it also divides and cripples the dominated classes as a whole. It makes us all less effective in our struggle for overall liberation.

Every woman deals with constant threats and attacks on body, mind and spirit. This society creates an atmosphere designed to terrorize and psychologically foot-bind us. Not only do these experiences inflict emotional trauma, they also commandeer and waste the time and energy of women, including those involved in the struggle for proletarian revolution.

In our organizations, if we don't treat one another as human beings, as comrades, then we won't be able to function collectively at an optimal level. Oppressive behavior must be concretely addressed whenever it becomes an obstacle to our struggle — crushed as quickly and decisively as possible without obsessing over it, so we can all move on to work on our fundamental task. Measures might include exposing, isolating, or no longer working with an offender who doesn't change. They might include actively protecting and defending those under threat.

Capitalism has many facets of evil; we have a lot of things we have to fight. Various forms of oppression are included in this. We have to be tough and determined, all of us, to not tolerate any harmful behavior in our ranks, while keeping our overall goals always in mind. We need more than equal rights, equal treatment, equal pay, equal assets, equal opportunity, egalitarian language, safe spaces. We need total emancipation for all the inhabitants of the Earth.

WHY CORRECT THEORY IS IMPORTANT

HYPOTHESIS:
A bean & cheese taco is good, but I can make an even tastier one with liver & peppermint.

From the day we're born, women are under intense pressure to be submissive, quiet, pleasing, nurturing, accommodating, weak and passive. We must overcome this social conditioning to assert ourselves, to take our place in the struggle. Fighting to be effective revolutionaries, to assert our interests in our organizations and in other areas of our lives can be difficult, unpleasant and exhausting. It's a long-term, active process that requires intense effort. But it's good for us—it makes us stronger. We have to become extremely strong if we hope to be able to fight this massive, ruthless, global system. In any case, we have no real choice. We can become what we need to be only by being it, within the field and process of struggle.

We have to develop our capacity to insist that our voices are heard, to make our social power felt. This must be a collective effort within our broad movement—to assert ourselves not in competition with one another, but to mutually assist each other to magnify our collective strength. My strength is your strength, and vice versa. The source of our strength as individuals, when we work together for our common goals, is the strength of our movement. Any orientation other than this will devolve into sectarianism, competition, individualism, elitism, and disunity—and will ensure our defeat.

We need to mutually support and strengthen all of us on the side of the people, the popular masses. We need to back each other up, not tear each other down. Any disagreements among us are secondary at this time (our primary antagonism is against the system)—and so we can have great diversity within our overall unity. Our unity doesn't have to be (and can't be) complete or comfortable—it exists for this specific historical moment, to get us past a specific conjuncture and remove our biggest obstacle, which we can only do together. In the process, we can deal with other contradictions and solve other problems (and there are plenty).

When we have that larger vision of total emancipation, when we focus our lives — all we desire and work for — on that, then our attitudes and practices that are a hindrance to us fall away in the process of common struggle. Then we are comrades, and the social categories we belong to become much less relevant. And the basis for them to one day totally disappear will be contingent upon our collective success.

Racism: the enemy's social tool

The oppression of social categories of people, whether defined as caste, race, gender, sex, sexual orientation or expression, religion, immigration status or others, isn't mainly a personal ideological problem (though it is also that). It's a social ideological tool wielded by dominant classes (in capitalism or any other type of class-divided social formation) to accomplish several things:

1) to justify practices in the pursuit of wealth that would otherwise be universally resisted as insanely cruel if done to humans (or any sentient beings), but since the "other" is dehumanized and objectified, it is rationalized as acceptable,

2) to force particular sections of the masses into more extreme situations of servitude and exploitation to maximize profit, and

3) to cement divisions among the dominated classes so as to weaken our ability to transform society.

In the US, the concept of race (a social construct with no biological basis) has been fluid, applied to various nationalities and arbitrarily defined categories of people in different ways at different times, in order to justify treating people as less than human.

Starting with the genocide of indigenous people and moving through slavery and all the way to today's "war on terror," and in countless other instances in between, race and racism have been used to excuse the ultra-violent policies that serve the accumulation of capital, and to gain the compliance of those groups not targeted or who are offered certain comparative advantages.

Identity politics are a form of reformism, which is the ideology of the petit bourgeoisie. They defend their class privileges, while also wanting everyone to be able to enjoy them. This is a source of the liberal, populist (non-class-based) call for "equality" within the system's framework.

The demand and desire for equality and justice are righteous. These are positive, progressive goals. Fighting for them can strengthen the unity of the popular masses, and help get us closer to total social transformation.

But this doesn't go far enough. The root of the problem must be addressed.

The solution to racism often offered by the petit bourgeoisie is for individuals or institutions to stop being racist. Like other reformist solutions, individually refraining from racist and other oppressive behavior and language is, though absolutely necessary, insufficient. Adjusting institutional policies is likewise insufficient.

Reformists always attempt to constrain resistance into paths and forms that may make them feel virtuous but won't actually ever win. Their efforts to mitigate specific forms of oppression may succeed, but capitalism can survive that. It can accommodate and adapt to "equality and justice" for any particular social category while still reproducing and enforcing class domination. Meanwhile oppression itself will remain in the capitalist toolbox, and it will be used, inevitably, on someone.

We can't end oppression without uprooting the entire foundation upon which it is based, the underlying social conditions that perpetuate and feed off of it: the division of humanity into different classes, and class domination.

Many are reluctant to face that. They would like to imagine that they can create an egalitarian situation by changing their own or others' behavior, rather than making the kinds of sacrifices necessary for the waging of class war. It's not in the economic interests of the petit bourgeoisie to overturn the whole social structure, and so they don't really want to. In politics as on the job, they're prepared to offer service, support and improvements. Not revolution.

Petit bourgeois progressives who truly want to eliminate all forms of oppression must repudiate their own class interests, and be willing to fight capitalism and imperialism, in alliance with and under the leadership of the proletariat.

Class domination is not classism.

Intersectionality theory offers the concept of a grid of oppressions with intersecting points. It proposes class as a category of oppression. But though these struggles are bound up together, they are

If you beg in just the right way, maybe I would change.
How's this?
PETITION
Please Please pretty please Stop Being so Evil

not equivalent. Class is not an identity — and class struggle is not a struggle against "classism." It is not an effort to end hatred or discrimination between members of different classes, or to win equal rights. (As the saying goes, members of all classes are already equally forbidden to steal bread).

Class is not simply another form of oppression. Class is qualitatively different. Under capitalism, class domination underpins the rest; it determines the way everything else is manifested in these times. It is domination structured as a whole matrix of social relations, in the economic, political and ideological fields, all ultimately determined by the economic: the process of exploitation of labor in the production of surplus value, which is the core mechanism of capitalism.

Class domination keeps the system running; class emancipation is the only thing that can stop it. Instead of aiming to puncture one of its tires, we need to crack the engine. In the capitalist era, the fundamental contradiction in society is between capital and labor. The reason it's important to identify society's fundamental contradiction is so that we can focus our efforts at its most vital spot and break it apart. We can move beyond capitalism only if that specific contradiction is pushed through to resolution, ending in the destruction of capital.

Where we locate the fundamental contradiction of the society determines our strategy, which in turn determines our daily priorities. We need to concentrate on where we can have the most impact, the highest potential to destroy the entire social system, a system that encompasses, but is larger than, any one of its many particular evil aspects.

Revolution doesn't solve everything.

With all that said, the long-term goal of a totally classless society has many steps that will inevitably fall short of that. The defeat and expropriation of the capitalist class by the working class is but one major step or key nodal point (manifested by revolution) — one that is necessary and may be achievable in our historical era. It does not mean that classes and oppression would be at once eliminated, but it would open a door to that possibility in a way that the rupture of any other social contradiction could not do.

A victorious proletarian revolution will not mean that we will automatically achieve utopia. After this major turning point, there will be continuing social antagonisms and continual struggle, including class struggle. The effort to break down and fully eliminate classes and all forms of domination will likely take generations.

Fighting oppression must not be postponed until after the victory of the working class over capital. At the same time, we need to recognize that a total end to oppression cannot be achieved, or separated out from, eliminating classes.

HOW TO MAKE A LEAFLET THAT SUCKS

VOTE TO OPPOSE BILL 52-3B AGAINST DIVESTMENTS FOR CORPORATE RESOURCE INCREASE

ACT NOW TO PREVENT THIS HORRIBLE OUTRAGE!!

HEADLINE THAT TAKES MORE THAN 5 SECONDS TO UNDERSTAND ←

1 COLUMN OF 7-POINT TYPE ←

NARROW MARGINS ←

GENERIC SLOGAN ←

- NO IMAGES
- NO WHITE SPACE
- NO CONTACT INFORMATION
- WHO PUT THIS THING OUT, ANYWAY, AND WHAT THE HELL DO THEY WANT?

Strengthen collectivity: combat individualism

Individualism is the ideology of competition, of capitalism. It consists of prioritizing one's perceived immediate personal interests above collective interests, and being blind to the fact that one's long-term personal interests actually correspond to the interests of the whole. This leads people to behave in ways that are detrimental to the collective, and ultimately to each individual as well.

Under capitalism, society does not meet the needs of the people, and we are structurally prevented from meeting our needs collectively. Capitalism's engine is competition. There is competition between classes as well as within classes. Within the working class, the capitalist system pits each person (or family) against all others in a struggle for survival.

Humans are social animals who, before agriculture arose and society was divided into classes, lived in bands. Our species evolved with a natural tendency to cooperate. But when people living under capitalism attempt to express this tendency, they are sharply discouraged. For example, when strangers spontaneously assist one another after a disaster, they are quickly dispersed and ordered to leave this task to the state.

Individualism is a powerful ideological weapon that the capitalist class uses to crush the subjectivity of the working class, and thus to prevent the potential liberation of the world from capitalist rule. Individualism is promoted and fortified by every possible cultural and economic means. We are indoctrinated from birth. Parents are compelled to teach their children to survive in the competitive framework (which they have no choice about living in) by "getting ahead," to "look out for number one," to put oneself in the best position possible (i.e., through education, or seeking a rich mate) to accumulate wealth for personal security.

Individualism is the ideology of the petit bourgeoisie (those who circulate capital by selling either services or goods, who tend to aspire to belong to the ruling class). It manifests itself as the striving for market power, for personal advancement, for comforts, for security and stability within the framework of the system. In contrast, proletarian ideology seeks to overturn the capitalist system and meet our needs collectively. But capitalism has been able to indoctrinate even members of the working class in petit bourgeois ways of thinking, to manipulate them into acting against their own interests, in ways that benefit capitalists instead.

Revolutionary militants are no less subject to ideological domination than anyone else. The difference is that they are consciously aware of it, to varying degrees, and thus are able to combat it. In order to fight the system, we must fight its dominant ideologies at every level: in society as a whole, in our organizations, and in our own individual hearts and minds.

This is an active and constant process of struggle. It will continue even after the ruling class has been defeated politically — we are so deeply conditioned that it may take generations to uproot their poisonous ideas. Ultimately, it will require that we construct a society (an economy, in particular) that retains no structural or social mechanism for rewarding individualism.

We should not be ashamed to discover individualism in our own hearts, or shame others for manifesting it — it is inevitable in capitalist society. Instead, the way to fight it is to bring it to light, examine it in relation to our overall political goals, and then consciously reject it (over and over again, as it will constantly re-arise).

Ideological strength requires an underpinning of political unity; these advance together. The motive for struggle on the ideological front is not to serve some abstract morality, but to achieve a specific political goal.

Individualism is not the same as individuality. Combatting individualism does not mean that everyone must be identical (which is impossible anyway) or that anyone should suppress their own thoughts, desires, or particular characteristics. On the contrary, we must recognize the value of each individual as inherent, and at the same time as it relates to the collective. Each person has specific strengths to contribute to our common work, and these should be enhanced and supported. Our weaknesses should be shared so we can help each other overcome them. We appreciate diversity and differences among us, which contribute to a dynamic social/political life, increasing our range of possibilities in action and thought. (In fact, for any motion to occur at all, in a dialectical process, differences are required, by definition). In groups, as in any aspect of the natural world, diversity ensures resilience, flexibility, adaptability, and evolution.

In order to struggle against individualism, we must recognize its manifestations. In political organizations, there are many ways that this destructive ideology materializes. They include (not exclusively) these 12 common types:

1) **Misplaced priorities.** Nothing is as important and urgent as crushing capitalism. Nothing. Countless lives will continue to be destroyed until we accomplish this task. The future existence of all life on Earth is at risk as long as this system exists. Everything we do should be, in some way, in service to our cause. Of course our basic needs must be met, which beyond self-reproduction

(subsisting) also include maintaining one's health and balance (mental, emotional, physical, social and cultural). These should support and renew our capacity to contribute to revolution. Even if we eliminate frivolous activities from our lives, we still have to make difficult choices about how we spend our time, because the system keeps us very busy in our effort to survive and meet our responsibilities. (This overload serves capitalism by making us too overwhelmed to resist). Therefore we have to constantly evaluate how much energy we give to particular activities, make correct choices even when they are painful, and order our lives in favor of the revolutionary struggle.

2) **Competition among ourselves.** This can involve using one's experience, knowledge, accomplishments, abilities or personality to gain personal power or prestige, and to repress the collective will. Instead, we should all strive to strengthen our collective democratic functioning by assisting each comrade to express her/himself, to overcome weaknesses, build strength, and maximize participation. We should struggle among ourselves within a framework of overall unity, in order to discover the truth together, and not attempt to impose one's own will over others (whether their disagreements are verbalized or silent), or monopolize any aspect of work. Individual power without collective power is useless and can never defeat our enemy.

3) **A lack of commitment.** In order to increase consumption of commodities, capitalist society obsessively pushes self-indulgence as an ideal. ("Because you're worth it.") It has created concepts of "comfort," "fun" and "satisfaction" that correspond to their economic need for us to buy things. Whatever doesn't please us in the moment, we are encouraged to abandon and replace. This leads to a market-based approach to life, including toward nature, love, spirituality, political work, and everything else. Unfortunately, political work is not comfortable, fun, and

instantly gratifying in the ways that we are conditioned to desire. Instead it is challenging, complex, and requires immense persistence. When this fact is discovered, a common response is to abandon it.

4) **Laziness.** Some people believe they've performed a great deed by joining an organization and declaring support for the cause. They stop here, congratulating themselves and posting revolutionary quotations all over Facebook. But this is like confusing the starting point in a marathon with the finish line. We can't stand on unearned laurels, but have to run the full distance: to do the hard work of constructing theory, defining a political line, and building organizations—pushing ourselves through to victory and beyond.

5) **Passivity.** Letting others always take the lead, and refusing to take initiative (once a collective approach has been decided) is an avoidance of responsibility. Each person should strive to participate and contribute to the maximum of her/his potential, to express ideas without fear, and be willing to do whatever work is necessary.

6) **Hero/martyr complex.** While it's essential to work to one's maximum capacity and strive to increase it, it can be tempting to overestimate what one's capacity actually is. A juggler with too many eggs will drop some of them. Similarly, taking on too many tasks and making too many commitments will result in failure to carry all of them out. Unreliability leads to uncertainty and paralysis for the other members of an organization, who have interconnected tasks that depend on one another for success. In addition, it could cause the person to burn out, rendering them totally ineffective. Instead of attempting personally to handle every task, we should help others share responsibilities. We have to accept that some tasks will not be accomplished (as well or at all)

until sufficient collective capacity is built.

7) **Defensive/aggressive ego.** In a collective endeavor, criticism should never be personal; thus there is no reason to be personally offended by it. We should not only be willing to listen to criticism with an open mind, but to welcome constructive criticism, and learn to evaluate our own work in the spirit of understanding our weaknesses in order to overcome them. Criticism of the work of a comrade or ally should always be offered in a constructive manner, with the intention of assisting their work. An alternative should be suggested along with it. We should not pick each other apart for every small mistake (which can be very demoralizing), but focus on fundamental issues.

8) **Self-expression.** Intellectuals (especially in academia) attempt to generate novel ideas for professional or "personal branding" purposes, rather than focusing on constructing theory to concretely assist class struggle. This is theory for theory's sake, or intellectualism. This practice converts theory into just another commodity, a gift to our enemy. The way to combat this is to produce our ideas (in whatever form) collectively. For artists, the concept of "art for art's sake" is a way to justify creating work without political or social content. This means squandering one's creativity and skills by offering them for the benefit of the ruling class, instead of for the working class. Intellectuals and artists should participate in other areas of political work, or they won't fully understand their subjects.

9) **Self-esteem.** Working hard is good, but not so good if there is an underlying motive of elevating one's own social position or being the center of attention. We do not need to build our self-esteem by seeking admiration, praise and flattery. Our self-respect and sense of connection should come from being an effective social agent for our class, connected to countless others within

a historical process. We should appreciate one another as comrades, and let each other know when we're doing good work, but not be motivated by a desire for public recognition.

10) **Friend sourcing.** Because of the atomization of our society, and consequent feelings of isolation, sometimes people join and use organizations as a means to alleviate loneliness, to make friends or develop relationships, whereas it should be the other way around: allowing friendships to arise from a foundation of political unity. If the personal aspect of a relationship is made primary over the political aspect, this can interfere with political functioning. Political agreement or disagreement can be falsely based on emotion. Underlying conflicts can manifest as personal attacks hidden under the guise of political disagreements, picking quarrels, harassment, or avoidance of common work because of discomfort. This creates a negative atmosphere which can sidetrack people's attention and undermine group cohesion. There is no room for drama in political organizations. We should focus on our overall goal, and be good comrades first, friends second.

11) **Liberalism.** Tolerating destructive behavior because one doesn't like conflict or want to "rock the boat," allows that behavior to continue and increase. Manifestations of liberalism include gossiping behind people's backs instead of bringing up problems collectively, failing to take opportunities to assert revolutionary ideas in appropriate situations, witnessing (or being subject to) oppressive acts or speech without saying anything, failing to hold comrades accountable, supporting or attacking views based on feelings about the person expressing them, and tolerating mediocrity in our work. These all result in an unprincipled peace that can lead to group apathy.

12) **Going off the rails.** The members of a revolutionary organization act only within the framework of political unity. Strength

comes from disciplined collectivity, and individual initiative must be based on this foundation. Taking action as an individual in ways that have no relationship to collectively agreed-upon strategy or goals can be dangerous. For example, committing an illegal act (impulsively or from a concealed plan) without the knowledge and agreement of the collective, puts others at risk, damages collective work, and destroys mutual trust. Failing to take the safety of the organization seriously and to abide by its security protocols is inexcusable.

Everything in capitalist society is geared to stop us from organizing to fight for revolution. We feel constant pressure to cave in to individualism. We are tempted with possibilities for self-advancement if we abandon the struggle, or are threatened with the opposite if we don't fall in line. If we insist on rejecting individualism, this can cost us our jobs. Friends may tell us we're crazy, boring, or depressing to talk to. Our family members might tell us that we are failing in our responsibilities to them when we devote time to political work. On TV and in movies, we are given poisonous models of human behavior.

Resisting all these influences is class struggle on the ideological front. We have to keep our bearings, pick our battles wisely, and refuse to kneel down under pressure. In our organizations, we must assist one another to overcome individualism and all enemy influences.

CONCLUSION

If the rate of production of commodities exceeds the speed of the natural renewal of materials, then expansion will inevitably hit physical limits. That is occurring now. But capital has no choice but to violate those limits, to expropriate and extract until it incorporates everything and wipes out all alternatives. This is its inexorable drive, and if unchecked, it will lead to omnicide. There is no escaping this inevitability, unless capitalism is defeated by the class that is in fundamental opposition to it, the working class.

It is in the interests of all the dominated classes (and those not yet assimilated into the global economy) to resist all forms of capitalist expropriation and resource extraction, and to build solidarity to fight the various forms these atrocities take. Resistance is necessary in that it aligns all the popular masses against capitalism. It strengthens our unity and fighting capacity. But resistance alone will not halt the process. Capital will respond with ever-increasing violence and, as it has repeatedly shown, will not hesitate at committing massacres on any scale, including genocide.

We do need to fight all the nightmare effects of capitalism, such as dispossession and ecocide. But the only way to win, to actually overcome capitalism, to wipe it out, is to focus our energy on its fundamental internal contradiction, capital vs. labor, and pushing that to its resolution, in our interests: to stop the reproduction of capital. This requires revolution led by the autonomous working class to overthrow the state, and to seize the means of production. Only the self-emancipation of the working class can release social production from the drive to accumulate. Only that can allow us, collectively, to organize production in a way that is rational and in harmony with the interests of humanity and the Earth.

For now, our enemy is stronger than we are. We have to overcome that, and meanwhile deal with the fact that if we begin to be effective, they will commit any conceivable atrocity to crush us. But we are potentially stronger than them. We outnumber them, and have right on our side.

Our immediate task is to increase our capacity, to build the organizations that together can be powerful enough to overcome the capitalists' accumulated forces of lies, wealth and arms. When we organize ourselves, we will be unstoppable.

An anti-capitalist/anti-imperialist movement is struggling to come into being as a social force. It can only do so if we take responsibility for embodying it, giving it form by becoming, ourselves, progressive and revolutionary militants. Emancipation is possible, and, more to the point, necessary for the survival and well-being of all life on Earth. It's up to us to make it happen.

Our sisters and brothers are rising up in many places, fighting and dying in struggle. Each of us must choose which side we're on. Attempting to remain uninvolved won't fly, because neutrality doesn't exist in an extremely polarized situation such as the one we are currently in. Refusing to enter the battlefield has the effect of serving the system.

Our expressions of solidarity mean nothing unless we're striving as hard as we can to organize ourselves and build our capacity to fight alongside our comrades internationally to defeat our common enemy.

You may feel isolated or surrounded by hostility, but you are not alone. We are part of a proud movement that spans the globe and all of human history — those who dedicate themselves to the cause of classless social relations on a healthy, thriving planet,

a mutually supportive and enhancing arrangement where each contributes to the common good, and the needs of all are met.

We must stay strong and focused. We can't compromise or sell ourselves or our struggle at any price. We have one chance to live and die—let's serve something worthy.

This is the work that gives our lives purpose and meaning. Nothing else is as important.

Unless we quickly defeat and overcome global capitalism, we're all going to die together, and badly. The entire possibility of any future for the planet will be cut short. All will be lost. The time has come for those of us who understand this to come together and do what is necessary.

Taking action itself reveals new possibilities we can not anticipate. What seems impossible will become reality because of our intervention. We must step decisively into that unknown.

HATING CAPITALISM:
It's a hobby. A sport. A way of life.

PART 1

50 WAYS TO PREPARE FOR REVOLUTION

We are currently unprepared to seize a revolutionary moment. We must fix that. How can we raise our levels of revolutionary consciousness, organization and struggle?

Raise consciousness

1) Raise consciousness with the purpose of raising the level of struggle.
2) Investigate before forming opinions.
3) Research how the world and the system work.
4) Read foundational and historical writings about revolution, by those who have experienced and led them.
5) Analyze the system's current condition and trajectory.
6) Learn about the resistance, uprisings and revolutions going on in the world today.
7) Read and evaluate the material that currently active groups are issuing and discussing.
8) Continuously develop ideology, theories and strategies for our movement.
9) Articulate our ideas.
10) Listen and speak in the spirit of mutual clarification.
11) Participate in discussion, to develop our ideas and hone our skills in expressing them, and to help others do so.
12) Figure out how to use all our various talents, positions, energy and resources as effectively as possible, to expose the system's evil, unredeemable and unreformable nature.
13) Analyze and explain the many ways the system dominates and exploits.
14) Exercise patience in winning over reluctant potential allies and supporters.
15) Ridicule and discredit the enemy.
16) Blog, comment, post information, and write leaflets, pamphlets and books about the enemy's crimes.

17) Exchange ideas locally, nationally and (within the law or safe channels) internationally.
18) Encourage others to participate in the revolutionary process.
19) Raise consciousness as a method of building organization.

Organize

20) Organize as a way to raise consciousness more broadly.
21) Start with people we know.
22) If our friends discourage us, make new friends.
23) Network sensibly with people online.
24) Find a group that we basically agree with. Work with it.
25) If there's no local group we want to work with, start one.
26) Find local people online who express similar ideas, and meet with them.
27) Write a leaflet with contact info. Pass it out in public to find potential comrades.
28) When we meet people, assess our points of agreement.
29) If we agree on basic essentials, decide how to work together. If not, say goodbye for now.
30) Build organization and ties locally, regionally and nationally.
31) Define allies according to overall outlook and goals.
32) Don't let secondary differences prevent cooperation.
33) Handle differences between allies non-antagonistically.
34) Refrain from saying anything aloud, on the phone or electronically that we wouldn't want to hear played back in court.
35) Keep illegal drugs away from our political life.
36) Research and practice good security culture.
37) Prioritize the wellbeing of our organizations over any personal considerations.
38) Organize in order to wage struggle.

Struggle

39) Use struggle to build organization.

40) Collectively determine what we want.

41) Articulate demands.

42) Act as far as possible within our capacity, not either below or beyond our capacity.

43) Assert our rights.

44) Defend and encourage our allies.

45) As opportunities arise, weaken the enemy and its ability to rule.

46) Obey the small laws. Don't get taken out of the game for something unworthy.

47) Refrain from illegal activities unless you'd trust your comrades with your life (because you are).

48) Avoid being distracted and diverted into symbolic action-for-action's sake.

49) Don't expect the enemy to act against its nature.

50) Turn every attack by the enemy into an opportunity to speak and organize.

I hate the way that if you organize effectively against capitalism, they kill you.
I hate that before you eat a carrot, you have to have an anxiety attack wondering if it's genetically modified, contaminated with lead, or whether you properly washed off all the pesticides.
Febreeze products.
You win.
PART 2

BRIEF DEFINITIONS
OF CONCEPTS

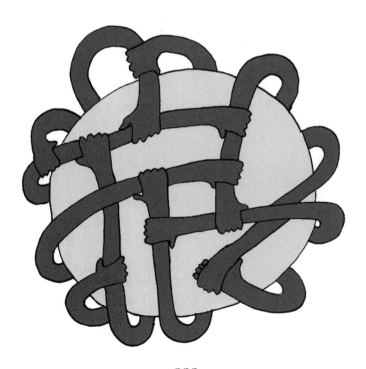

Brief definitions:

These definitions are extremely limited and constantly evolving. Our interpretations of reality are always constrained by the boundaries of our own thinking; in addition they can never catch up to reality itself, which is ever-changing.

These are not in alphabetical order, by the way, but in a logical chain best read from beginning to end.

Mode of production: The matrix of social relations (economic, political, ideological) that defines the nature of a social formation, determined by the dominant ways that items for social consumption are produced, accumulated and distributed. Capitalism is the dominant mode of production in the world today, the current development of 10,000+ years of class-divided society.

Social formation: All of the internal contradictions within the structures and practices (economic, political, ideological) comprising a coherent group system that reproduces itself in a constant dynamic of construction and destruction. Social formations include nations, businesses, families, etc.

Capitalism: a mode of production in which the social product is produced through the exploitation of workers as they convert natural materials into commodities through the application of labor power, plus the private ownership of the means of production and private appropriation of surplus value by non-producers (capitalists).

Classes: Dynamic social forces engaged in struggle determined by the antagonistic relations of production. The fundamental contradiction under capitalism is labor vs. capital, which is manifested by constant struggle between the two fundamental and polarized classes: the working class and the capitalist class. This struggle occurs within a matrix of economic, political and ideological relations (ultimately determined by the economic). (This is in contrast to a sociological view of classes that categorizes individuals using specific criteria or attributes, such as income).

Economic base: The economy of any class-divided social formation consists of the combination of and relations between producers (labor power), the means of production, and non-producers (who appropriate surplus product).

Superstructure: The dominant ideology plus the institutions and exercise of political power, that together justify, sustain, support, protect, and perpetuate the economic base.

Social surplus: Wealth or products that are not consumed by a social formation (society), nor are necessary for its reproduction, but can be used for exchange (trade) with other social formations.

Use-value: The quality of fulfilling a need. Many things have use value but no exchange value (examples: fresh air, intuition, a hug, a haircut, a family meal). The number of these is dwindling as capitalism relentlessly strives to impose exchange value on everything. For example, potable water no longer makes the list.

Exchange value: Standardized worth in the context of the market, relative to the worth of other items it can be traded for.

The Labor Theory of Value: The exchange value of a product is based on the socially necessary amount of labor power (measured in time) that is generally required to produce it. For example, if one person spends an hour catching a fish, they might trade it for an amount of blueberries it took an hour to collect.

Absent other factors, it wouldn't make sense to trade the results of a day's worth of fishing for the results of an hour's worth of blueberry picking.

Commodity: A product manufactured primarily for its exchange value, from natural materials using human labor power. (Its use value is secondary, required only enough to make it sellable, i.e.: someone has to feel a need to buy it). Commodities are fungible, which means they're standardized for the purposes of exchange, and have little or no qualitative variation (one ton of steel is reliably similar to another ton of steel). Examples of commodities are grains, lumber, iPads, fuels, currencies, frozen waffles, and labor power itself (sold by the worker in units of time).

Expropriation/extraction (aka: original, primary or primitive accumulation): Obtaining control of natural resources to continuously feed the productive process. This is done through various coercive means of dispossession, from conquest and overt theft to more subtle forms of domination and extortion. Examples include invading a country and seizing their forests or oil fields, dumping grain to ruin farmers and then buying their land at fire-sale prices, using eminent domain to obtain drilling rights under someone's land, and using drag nets in non-territorial ocean waters.

Surplus Value: The residue of the social process (involving the economic, political and ideological spheres) of capitalist production, which manifests as the theft of labor power (exploitation) during the conversion of natural materials into commodities. Only human labor power produces new, material surplus value. The buyer of labor power (the capitalist) appropriates the surplus value generated in the process of commodity production.

Reduced to its economic essence, surplus value is the portion of exchange value of a commodity that exists as labor power crystallized in it. The capitalist pays workers less than the value of what they produce. What's left after paying their wages, and after paying fixed costs such as machinery and inputs, is surplus value. (If sold to a retailer, an additional amount will be added to the price of the final sale, which is not surplus value but mercantile profit).

Capitalists can pay less than labor power is worth because of the relations of production: their private ownership and control over the means of production, which forces the working class to sell their labor power for survival. Private ownership is accepted by the members of a society because of a combination of ideological domination (the cultivation of belief in the "right" to private property) and coercive force.

Capital: The social (economic, political, ideological) process of the production of surplus value. It is ever-expanding because surplus value must be re-invested and becomes new capital. The production of surplus value is how capital reproduces itself.

Profit: The revenue accumulated through an exchange of values.

Surplus value and profit are not identical. Surplus value is the productive form of profit, which is crystallized as new material value. Profit can also be generated in other ways, which do not directly involve (though they do, as a whole, ultimately rest upon) commodity production. Non-productive profit (or fictitious value) is the result of the circulation of capital (in the form of interest, the sale of services, or unequal exchanges). Fictitious value becomes toxic when speculation overinflates it to a point that it can begin to destabilize an economy.

The production, accumulation and re-investment of surplus value is the essence and purpose of capitalism, the way that capital reproduces itself and multiplies. As it grows, capital pushes itself into every investment opportunity it can possibly locate within the global economy, and violently opens up new opportunities when necessary. When inevitable crises of overproduction occur, capital increasingly relies on non-productive (fictitious, and ever more toxic) means of self-reproduction (such as financial speculation), putting the system ever-deeper into an unsolvable predicament.

Philosophies and types of knowledge:

Idealism: the belief that the world is a projection of our mental activity, that the nature of reality is determined by ideas.

Postmodernism: the belief that each individual subjectivity creates its own reality.

Metaphysics: a purely speculative understanding of a phenomenon, not based on empirical knowledge or verifiable facts.

Mysticism: the belief in a reality that is beyond the ordinary perception of sentient beings.

Animism: the belief that the world is alive and comprised of interconnected subjectivities.

Class consciousness: an appropriation of the ideas corresponding to one's class interests.

Materialism: the belief that reality consists of matter in motion (which includes ideas, thoughts, emotions, intuition and other phenomena of the mind).

Empirical knowledge: based on perceptions and experience. Empirical knowledge is preliminary or embryonic, apprehending the surface level of a phenomenon.

Rational knowledge: the analysis and synthesis of empirical knowledge can help us grasp the underlying core nature of a phenomenon. As we define phenomena, the practice of rationalizing empirical knowledge is the opposite approach from relying on preconceived formulas or jumping to metaphysical conclusions. It helps us avoid pragmatism (which addresses effects and appearances rather than causes or internal contradictions).

There is a dialectical (mutually contradictory and interdependent) relationship between empirical and rational knowledge. Both kinds can be either direct (your own), or indirect (someone else's that you learn from). When enough empirical data is acquired, this lays the basis for rational understanding (quantitative change becomes qualitative).

Stephanie McMillan has been a political cartoonist since 1992. She is the creator of the editorial cartoon *Code Green*, and the comic strip *Minimum Security*, syndicated through Universal Uclick.

She is the author of six previous books. Her cartoons have earned several major awards, including the RFK Journalism Award (2012), and the Sigma Delta Chi Award from the Society for Professional Journalists (2010). They have appeared in hundreds of publications, anthologies and textbooks worldwide including the *Los Angeles Times, the South Florida Sun-Sentinel, Daily Beast, The Occupied Wall Street Journal, Funny Times,* and the *San Francisco Bay Guardian.*

Her cartoons have been included in numerous group exhibitions, including the Museum of Comic and Cartoon Art (New York), and the San Francisco Comic Art Museum. A solo show of her work was held in 2013 at the West Gallery, California State University, Northridge.

An organizer for most of her life, Stephanie is a founding member of the anti-capitalist/anti-imperialist group One Struggle. She also contributes political theory to Idées Nouvelles, Idées Prolétariennes. She is a dynamic public speaker, and has given presentations at the Left Forum, Sierra Summit, CUNY, and many other venues.

Photo by Sarah Cruz, Port-au-Prince, Haiti, October 2012.

ACKNOWLEDGEMENTS

This book owes a great debt to all those who read early drafts and provided corrections and valuable critiques, as well as those who pointed out instances that required elaboration or clarification. Rather than risk leaving anyone out of a long list of names, I offer my deep appreciation to all of you collectively.

Publication has been made possible through the funding of many generous supporters, including:

- Lu Allen

- Warren Bernard

- Rachael Charbonneau

- Deep Green Resistance

- Edmonton Small Press Association (ESPA)

- Amy Grieder

- Mark Hand

- D F Hawthorne

- John Kovalic

- Gardner Monks

- Malcolm Morrison

- Rob Rogers

Many thanks!

ABOUT INIP

INIP (Idées Nouvelles Idées Prolétariennes) is a publishing entity for the popularization of theory and other texts that serve the interests of the working class in our struggle against capital.

Purpose:

Proletarian class consciousness, the most necessary element of a revolutionary struggle, is currently nearly non-existent in most social formations. Our purpose is to influence objective conditions by addressing the subjective factor; in other words, to increase the potential for revolution by popularizing documents that consolidate and advance the theory of our class and assert a corresponding political line.

Method:

This project promotes the constructing of theory and political line through a constant dialectical process of unity-struggle-unity (defining initial unity and achieving a higher level of unity through struggle). While we recognize essential contributions from the past, proletarian theory is not a static dogma, but a living science. It is most powerful when collectively constructed and appropriated, for our class to advance together. Theory and line are perpetually subject to verification through practice, and to rectification as understanding develops.

www.koleksyon-inip.org
koleksyon.inip@gmail.com

We face two choices:
omnicide or global revolution.
Workers of the world: UNITE!